Tribute To
Teddy Bear Artists
by Linda Mullins
<u>Series 2</u>

(Left to right) *Parade.* 1995. 15-3/4in (40cm); cinnamon colored mohair; glass eyes; fully jointed. *Pablo.* 1995. 23-3/4in (60cm); brown wavy mohair; glass eyes; fully jointed. P.P. 150. 1995. 13in (35cm); light blonde mohair; shoe button eyes; fully jointed. P.P. 150's design was inspired by Steiff's early elephant button bears. *Photograph by Masato Tashir.*

Published by Hobby House Press, Inc.
Grantsville, Maryland 21536

DEDICATION

This book is affectionately dedicated to my friend Georgi Bohrod Rothe.

ACKNOWLEDGMENTS

I wish to thank all the artists featured in this publication, for without their kind cooperation and sharing of their bear making knowledge this book would not have become a reality. My heartfelt thanks to my dear friend Georgi Bohrod Rothe. Her sincere personal interest and professional contribution to this book were of great importance to me. Thanks also goes to my Editor Mary Beth Ruddell for her invaluable advice and patience, and also to Patricia Matthews whose company, Associated Business Services, provided the excellent computer service. To my publishers Gary and Mary Ruddell for their continued support and faith in me. Finally, no words can express the gratitude I have for the understanding and encouragement my husband Wally continues to give me.

ABOUT THE AUTHOR

Little did I know that when my wonderful husband Wally gave me my first antique bear 16 years ago, it would begin a lifelong love affair with Teddy Bears. Over the years, not only has my collection grown, but my true affection and respect for all those people who make up this wonderful world of Teddy Bear collecting and artistry.

My semi-annual *Linda's Teddy Bear, Doll & Antique Toy Show and Sale* is nearly entering its second decade. Held in my hometown of San Diego, California, the show continues to grow in popularity. More than 3000 people come to get acquainted and purchase bears from the 150 participating dealers at the two-day event held at the Scottish Rite Center. I am so fortunate to have made friends from America, Britain, Europe, Australia, and Japan who have exhibited at my show. Along with the exhibits, demonstrations, and guest appearances, I organize an artist competition called "The West Coast Crystal Artist Teddy Bear & Doll Competition." I am thrilled at the quality of participants which made award judging extremely difficult for these contests.

I am also proud to say that my shows help raise funds for Good Bears of the World (G.B.W.). Participating dealers and collectors at the show donate Teddy Bears for this non-profit organization to sell.

Another outgrowth of my love of Teddy Bears is a growing number of books which I have written. This book is the tenth which Hobby House has published. Sharing my experiences and knowledge of history, collecting and the Teddy Bear world, has given me the marvelous opportunities to open the archives of the Library of Congress in Washington, D.C. Also, Wally and I have been welcomed on tours and interviews with all the major bear manufacturers in America, Germany, and Britain.

The doors to fabulous shows have opened and invited me in. I have been able to participate in incomparable events such as Glenn and Irene Jackman's "British Teddy Bear Festival", Rob and Inge Kuiter's "Amerongen Bear Festival" in Holland; the Walt Disney World® Bear Conventions; the First Japan Teddy Bear Association's Show; and D.L. Harrison Teddy Bear Conventions in Baltimore, Maryland.

Most recently, you may have seen me on the QVC home shopping television network, talking about well-known Teddy Bear artists and manufacturers.

The most endearing moments of my involvement with bears are all the special people Wally and I have met over the years. This book is truly for all of my "beary" dear friends, those whom I already know and those whom I hope to meet along the way.

Front Cover: (Left) Joan Woessner — Bear Elegance Exclusives. *Juliana.* 1995. 20in (51cm); pale champagne colored distressed mohair; black glass eyes; mink eyelashes; fully jointed. (Right) Steve Schutt — Bears-"S"-Ence. *Kent.* 1995. 15in (38cm); honey colored distressed mohair, black glass eyes; fully jointed. Both bears were created for Linda by the artist especially for the cover of her book. *Photograph by Allen Carrasco — Carrasco Productions.*

Table of Contents: Top (Left to Right): *Keanu* by Pat Murphy — Murphy Bears; *Otis* and *Otis Major* by Patricia Gye — Wayfarer Bears; Tiny one-of-a-kind Bear by Kazuko Ichikawa. *Bottom* (Left to Right): *Crocsou* by Marylou Jouet — Joueteddy; *Broome With Alice Springs the Kangaroo.by* Jennifer Laing — Totally Bear; *Fight! Kobe by* Etsuko Hasegawa — Star Child Co., Ltd.

Back Cover: An appealing selection of Tammie Lawrence's *Teeny Tattered Teddys,* in Victorian pastel shades of distressed mohair. Produced in 1995, each bear is approximately 4in (10cm) tall, and fully jointed with black bead eyes. Limited edition of 300. *Photograph by George Comito.*

Tribute to Teddy Bear Artists, Series 2 is an independent study by the author Linda Mullins and published by Hobby House Press, Inc. The research and publication of this book were not sponsored in any way by the artists of the bears featured in this study.

The values given within this book are intended as value guides rather than arbitrarily set prices. The values quoted are as accurate as possible but in the case of errors, typographical, clerical or otherwise, the author and publisher assume no liability nor responsibility for any loss incurred by users of this book.

Additional copies of this book may be purchased at $29.95 (plus postage and handling) from

Hobby House Press, Inc.

1 Corporate Drive
Grantsville, Maryland 21536
1-800-554-1447
or from your favorite bookstore or dealer.

©1996 Linda Mullins

ISBN: 0-87588-456-3

Table of Contents

3

Chapter 1

THE INTERNATIONAL TEDDY BEAR SCENE

Making Teddy Bears by hand is no longer just a hobby; nor are the bears themselves simply a gift to keep a young child company. Fabricating handmade Teddy Bears has grown from a friendly avocation into a popular cottage industry. What began as a collector's opportunity to own wonderful replicas of expensive antique treasures has matured into a full-fledged artistic expression of soft sculpture masterpieces.

Bear artists themselves frequently possess a rare combination of creativity and business savvy. To be successful, a bear artist must master his/her craft and offer considerable innovation in conveying the gamut emotions, stature, and presence of one of this century's dearest expressions of warmth, love, and understanding — the Teddy Bear.

While the United States remains the primary home and breeding ground of this unique cultural trend, hand made Teddy Bear making is rapidly spreading around the world. Areas of noticeable growth are the United Kingdom, Australia, and Japan. However, plenty of other countries are gaining ground and are producing rare and exciting bears.

I invited a number of prominent editors, show promoters, and store owners to assist me in presenting an overview of artist Teddy Bears. A few countries are so new to the "bear world" that artists there work in near isolation, often traveling to other countries even to buy materials, much less exhibit their wares. What is included here are some of the many eloquent and informative responses received from around the world. I hope you enjoy the sampling which follows.

ONE WORLD

1. Teddy Bear artists around the world are known for their generosity in donating their creations for charitable events. This magnificent piece, *One World,* was created by American Teddy Bear artist Barbara Golden. *One World* was one of the donations made by more than 100 artists from around the world especially for "Berryman's International Teddy Bear Artists' Auction." The auction benefited the victims of the devastating earthquake that rocked Kobe and parts of Osaka, Japan on January 17, 1995. The auction raised ¥22 million (approximately $220,000), and *One World* commanded a price of ¥320,000 (approximately $3,200).

Stephen Cronk, Editor *Teddy Bear Review* (America)
"Originally a quarterly publication, *Teddy Bear Review* is issued six times a year and boasts a ...paid circulation of nearly 60,000....As the general public's interest in teddies has grown, along with the sophistication of those who make them and collect them, so has (the magazine) grown. The number of hobbyists and artists working today is phenomenal, and as some talented artists expand their businesses...they often hire others to help in production—becoming, themselves, manufactures of handmade bears. Some artists also design and create bears which are then sold to large manufacturers as prototypes for mass production."

2. Stephen L. Cronk is a familiar face at Teddy Bear events across the country. Editor of *Teddy Bear Review,* Stephen is also responsible for contributing to the success of the magazine's Annual Doll & Teddy Bear Expo.

David Miller, Publisher *Teddy Bear and Friends*® (America)

"From a publishing stand point, the constant game of reporting the activities of the Teddy Bear world to collectors is becoming more challenging every day. People from all corners of the world are learning the skills of bear making and experiencing the rewards. With every new artist comes a different approach, style, and story to tell....I have met computer programmers, police officers, nurses, teachers, lawyers...to name a few that have found true rewards with Teddy Bear making. Public service positions seem to be the most popular among Teddy Bear artists. Wanting to give and help others are common characteristics associated with Teddy Bear artists...the more I see and learn...the more unique every bear becomes. Teddy Bear making is no different than most art forms. The finished product becomes a reflection of the artist and their surroundings. The phenomena of Teddy Bear collecting and making is just beginning. The introduction of Teddy Bear figurines, affordable Teddy Bears from manufacturers, (a) growing world of artists, and enthusiastic collectors complete the formula for a long and healthy future for the Teddy Bear world."

3. In his quest to learn more about the growing world of Teddy Bear collecting and artistry, David L. Miller, publisher of *Teddy Bear & Friends*® magazine travels throughout America exhibiting at shows and meeting bear collectors.

Evelyn Penfield, President San Diego Teddy Bear Artist Club (America)

"The San Diego Teddy Bear Artist Club has over 80 members with a large attendance at monthly meetings...Much organization must be done by many members sharing their time, talent, ideas, and willingness to welcome new members. Because the membership is so diversified from famous to as yet unknown, from artist to appreciator, our club offers participation in three areas—social, educational, and philanthropic...Not only does our bear club offer friendship and encouragement, but also provides a vehicle for new artists to enter the competitive world of sales...by participating on the club sales table at (nearby shows)."

Jean Van Meeuwen-Slater, Bear Artist (Belgium)

"Belgium is a land sandwiched between Holland, Germany, France, and Luxembourg with two languages, Dutch and French. The Bear market is in its infancy here. There are only a few collectors; we have no show promoters as such. We are dependent on the Dutch show promoters who put on Doll and Bear Shows in the Flemish part of Belgium; we also are dependent on the Dutch Bear magazines. For Bear Shows, we have to travel to the U.K., Holland, and Germany. The collecting of bears is growing here but at a much slower pace than our neighbors."

4. Karl and Sheila Gibbons promote the work of Teddy Bear artists around the world through their wonderful Teddy Bear shop Theodore's Bear Emporium based at the Old Waiting Room, Mortlake Station, London.

Karl Gibbons, Store Owner Theodore's Bear Emporium (Britain)

"The UK is approximately the size of the state of Oregon and has a population of 58 million people compared to the 257 million in the USA. However, I believe that we are world leaders in the design and manufacture of the teddy, with companies including The Deans Rag Book Company, Britain's oldest manufacturer founded in 1903...The majority of artists still produce all the work themselves...Since 1990 the number of known Bear Artist's and makers in the UK has grown by an estimated 260%. The essential ingredient to any Teddy Bear is the raw materials and once again the UK is fortunate to have the world's premier mill, Norton's, for the production of mohair fabrics. This, together with excellent specialist supplies and coupled with our close geographical proximity to Germany, gives the UK artist access to the world's finest mohair, plush fabrics, components, and accessories. All this talent has lead to a thriving and developing UK teddy scene with over ...85+ shops...30 exclusive Teddy Bear shows...3 dedicated magazines...10 Teddy Bear clubs and 16 permanent museums."

5. Beatrijs van Westerop, publisher and editor of *BeerBericht to Teddy's,* personal love of Teddy Bears is exemplified in the quality and contents of her wonderful publication. Beatrijs is pictured affectionately holding a Stier Bear by the Amstel River in Amsterdam.

Beatrijs van Westerop, Publisher/Editor
BeerBericht to Teddy's (Holland)
"There are about 120 bear artists in Holland; about 50 of them are trying to make a living of their art. Apart from that there are about 300 people making bears at home. There is at least one bear show every weekend. Sometimes there are three shows held on the same day and Dutch bear people also attend shows in England and Germany as well. We are hosts to the annual competition and the annual Amerongen competition for bear makers. This year another major competition will be added: The Open European Teddy Bear Championships. The winners of the national contests in Holland, Germany, and England will compete, but other contestants are allowed to enter as well. In this way, it is still possible that relative outsiders may win the title, European Champion, in one of the various categories."

Jennifer Laing, Author, Artist, and Show Promoter (Australia and New Zealand)
"The Antipodean Bearmakers Co-op was founded in June 1991 as a non-profit association of professional bear artists from around Australia and New Zealand. To date it is the only group of its type in the Antipodes, or southern hemisphere. ...The original nucleus of the Co-op, comprised of 13 professional bear artists – myself, Michael and Judy Walton, Cindy Lowe, Gerry Warlow, June Kittlety, Loris Hancock, Kay VanderLey, Briony Nottage, Jenny Round, Winifred Belmont, Pat Tomlinson, and Pat Lovelock is the first of its kind in this part of the world. The first generation of bear artists are still displaying their talents in their ongoing work today. There are currently over 90 professional bear artists from all over Australia and New Zealand in the Co-op and it is still growing rapidly. (My) First Sydney International Bear Fair in September 1994 was a resounding success. Artists, bear authorities, antique dealers, retailers, and collectors came from all over the world to attend and share their knowledge in three days of seminars, workshops, competitions and trading, culminating in a charity auction dinner and an island picnic. The Fair helped put Australia on the world map for bears as it really sparked an interest in what is happening with the talent 'down-under.'"

Pat Rush, Editor *Hugglets* (Britain)
"The last few years have seen enormous changes in the Teddy Bear artist world in Britain. Five years ago, there were only a handful of artists. Now there are hundreds, with many turning a part-time hobby into a full-time business. There have been changes, too, in the bears themselves. The earliest artist bears were rarely dressed, for instance... a number of shops (still report) a resistance to dressed bears. Yet at specialist Teddy Bear fairs and at shops frequented by some of the most avid collectors, the carefully dressed and accessorized teddies are always in great demand....An even more significant change over the years has been in the sizes of the limited editions. Early editions tended to be very large, for the simple reason that artists were forced to buy mohair in complete roles of 30 meters. Now, they can buy a huge variety of fabrics in cut lengths...which has meant a huge increase in the number of small limited editions and of one-offs...Another relatively recent development is the large number of bear-making courses and workshops being held...The number of Teddy Bear fairs and of doll and teddy fairs, has increased dramatically over the past couple of years. Over 70 were planned for 1995, covering the whole country...Prices for artist bears vary enormously. Certainly, the recession has meant that many collectors have fewer pounds in their pockets, so there is a steady market for bears in the £40 - £60 (approximately $60 - $95) bracket. No doubt the recession has also contributed to the popularity of smaller and undressed bears...collectors will pay top price for a bear that they really covet. Beautifully dressed and accessorized bears can sell for anything from a hundred to many hundreds of pounds, depending on the intricacy of the design and the popularity of the artist. Some advice for aspiring artists: As a magazine editor, I am amazed at how few artists take the trouble to prepare even the simplest of publicity for their business. Editors are always looking for good photos...A good photo of a fairly good bear will stand far more chance of publication than a terrible picture of a superb creation. ..So, if you've won an award, created something out of the ordinary, or have some other news to report, don't just tell all your friends. Take a picture, write a few words about your achievement, and send it off to any newspaper or magazine that might be interested."

Beth Savino, Show Promoter and Store Owner, The Toy Store (America)
"We first introduced bears into our Toledo, Ohio show in 1980. That year Margarete Steiff GmBH entered the world of collecting with their Jubilee bear, affectionately known to collectors as *Papa*. With him came Hans-Otto Steiff, billed as "Steiff's Goodwill Ambassador." This wonderful man who had a genuine love of his product made numerous appearances at our shows, helping to add collectors of all ages to the fold. ...Early artists who attended the show and spread the word included Beverly Port, Ted Menten, and Carol-Lynn Rôssel-Waugh. Not only did they make bears, they told people about it. Another major force is Gary Ruddell (who) brought us authors, appraiser(s), and the DOTY® and TOBY® awards...Terry and Doris Michaud brought their collection for people to actually see and then began something new: the seminar. (Then) Jim Ownby told us about loving and caring with Teddy Bears. He and Ben Savino initiated the Toledo Den of Good Bears of the World, with Terrie Stong as Chairman. The man who first told us it was proper to still love our bear was Peter Bull...*Bully Bear* led the way for other artists and collectors to have their creations reproduced. Workshops became popular as bear collectors wanted to become bear makers. (Today) our show has all the fun of a Teddy Bear picnic, without the ants.""

Lyn Vowles, Editor *Teddy Bear Times* (Britain)
"...The British Bear Awards, the bear world's equivalent to the Oscars, attracts a record number of entries year by year. The judging can now take all day and preparation many long months. It is estimated that we have now more than 800 bear artists up and down the country. Some are newcomers, from every walk of life and from eight to eighty, inspired by those who have led the British charge.""

Marianne and Jürgen Cieslik, Authors, Publishers, and Show Promoters, Verlag Marianne Cieslik (Germany)
"Compared to America or England, the German bear artist scene is just growing up. The most popular type of bear is 70% whimsical, 30% nostalgic, dressed and made of only the best mohair in gold, beige, or cream. Only about ten artists have their own business, all others have their jobs or are married and sell bears as a hobby. The only show that exhibits just Teddy Bears is our *Teddybär Total*. There are several mixed with dolls. Collectors in Germany are interested in 50% artist bears, 10% contemporary bears, and 40% antique. Every year, our magazine *Teddybär und seine Freunde* does a competition with a different subject. This year "Teddybär Goes to Bearlywood" was very successful. The most popular range of bears is between DM 180 to DM 240 (approximately $250 - $325). Some very good artists ask for DM 800 (approximately $550) and more.""

6. Jürgen Cieslik promoter of the German Teddy Bear convention "Teddybär Total," hesitantly cuts the magnificent cake at a banquet celebrating the first occurrence of the event (April, 1995).

Kazundo Onozuka, Chairperson Japan Teddy Bear Association (Japan)
"The Japan Teddy Bear Association (JTBA) was established in 1993 as a non-profit organization to provide a medium for Japanese Teddy Bear fans to share their mutual interest. With a present total of over 1500 members, the JTBA is active in promoting the Teddy Bear world by assisting in exchanges between foreign artists and collectors, most significantly by sponsoring an annual convention in Tokyo. The JTBA also engages in charity and volunteer work. The Teddy Bear world in Japan is somewhat different from Europe and America. In Japan, the scarcity of antique collectibles has led Japanese collectors to seek out fine examples of contemporary artist's works. Therefore, the demand for artists' bears is steadily increasing. Also, most artists and collectors in Japan tend to be in their 20s and 30s."

7. Kazundo Onozuka, founder and chairperson of the Japan Teddy Bear Association (JTBA), has contributed greatly to the popularity and interest in Teddy Bears in Japan. It is his goal to educate and inform the Japanese collectors and artists about the international Teddy Bear scene through the Association.

Sandy Morrow, Show Organizer The Bear Fair (Canada)
"The Bear Fair is now three years old (first held in 1992). It is a three day event that features hands-on workshops, business education workshops for all Teddy Bear artists, a charity auction whose proceeds are donated to a local children's charity, and celebrity guest artists who each do a workshop. The show drew 1800 people in 1994 and we expect around 2000 this year, which is a very good sized crowd in these parts...I started the Bear Fair because I felt the Canadian artists were not getting the recognition they deserved. There was no real large scale event anywhere that was open to artists from across the country. ..there is an incredible pool of talent within Canada's teddy artist community. All types of bears seem really popular here. We are still educating the general public as to the value and durability of mohair as a medium for teds and so their higher price tag. Since the market is relatively new, the majority of our collectors are collecting artist bears. The prices are all over the map. 'Junior' artists are working in acrylic or mediums other than mohair and selling 6 to 24in (15cm—61cm) bears starting at $25. Good mohair teds usually start in the $60 - $70 range for 6in (15cm) bears. Good minis, under 4in (10cm) usually start at $50 and large mohair bears have sold for as much as $600 and up. ...I find the teddy artists warm and giving people. Many still have a fear of sharing because they have yet to recognize that there will never be enough Teddy Bears in the world to go around. Some advice for bear makers/marketers: 1) Before you take bears into any store, do your homework. Decide ahead of time what price you want for your bears; Cast the price in concrete and put the concrete block around your neck just so you won't forget yourself in the heat of negotiations; 2) Find out the store's usual practice; do they buy outright or do they take consignment? 3) When you get to the store, don't be swayed by any arguments to change (i.e., lower your price); 4) Don't let any retailer tell you where you can or cannot sell your bears outside their store. Moreover, don't let them tell you what price you can sell them for outside of the store. It isn't their call. It is yours."

Robin Rive, Artist and Owner Countrylife New Zealand (New Zealand)
"In spite of a small population of only 3,500,000 people, the Teddy Bear scene is very alive in New Zealand with the teddy tradition going back to Edwardian times. There are many "old-world" country-style gift shops that specialize in Teddy Bears, bear accessories, and bear making kits. Bear-making classes are extremely popular. New Zealand has about 30 bear artists and many keen amateur makers. Innovative artists use hand-dyed and felted wool, natural wool, as well as traditional mohair and man-made fabrics. Annual Teddy Bear picnics are popular throughout the country.

American Bear Artists

Chapter 2

Lori Baker
L. BAKER & CO.

One of my main achievements in life is really turning my bear and hare making into a full time business. I have been able to support myself and my son after a divorce, doing something I love and I am very proud of that!

My bears are quite lazy. They can't stand up. I make about 700 of them a year and sell them for $195 to $240 apiece. Mostly they are open-ended as far as the line goes, but I do change designs often. A few one-of-a-kinds also find their way in. I have a fairly good wholesale business going, so I only do two to four shows a year. I also exhibit at a Folk Art Trade show twice a year.

My mother, Eileen, (who taught me how to sew soft toys) sews and helps me tremendously. My neighbor, Debbie, is irreplaceable as she does all of my cutting. They're both great and I depend on them a lot.

I've been making bears for more than 20 years and selling them for nine. At first, paying my dues by doing "sooo" many shows and being on the road was hard. But it was worth it!

8. Lori Baker's creations are just a little different than the average artist. Lori says they are lazy and they can't stand! However, this nontraditional look obviously appeals to collectors since Lori's work is in high demand.

9. *Pinocchio.* 1995. 19in (48cm); white mohair head and paws; red mohair appliquéd cheeks; cloth body; black wool felt feet; glass eyes; unjointed arms and legs; swivel head. Note: extra long nose; doll style of bear.

9

Jody A. Battaglia
beary best friends®

My bears are antique-like reproductions that are filled with excelsior and stressed (and no, they are not nervous) for a vintage look. Then they are dressed for the period. At first, I made bears for my son. I started selling bears, gnomes, and other toys in 1979 and the bears very quickly took over.

Until very recently I did everything by myself. This year (1995) I asked my mother, Gloria Balaban, to sew the little toys the bears hold. That's quite appropriate since she taught me to sew at a young age and always encouraged me to explore my imagination. I've recently asked a friend to help sew the body parts...but not the head. My husband cuts out the bears.

I manage to make approximately 500 bears a year and, now that my children are older, attend eight shows a year. The shows are basically my retail outlet and I also fill orders from home. The only place I wholesale to is "The Magpie's Nest" in Canterbury, England.

My price range is from $55 to $150, with sizes ranging from 5 — 14in (13 — 36cm). I think that pricing is the most difficult segment of the bear making business. My goal has always been to keep my work affordable. I want to make it so I myself could afford to buy it.

One of the things I truly love about my "job" is preparing for a show and playing with my bears as I fill basket upon basket of them. Perhaps it sounds silly, but it gives me so much pleasure.

10. Jody Battaglia has designed a line of bears that are easily recognizable by their cute character faces and appealing outfits. An additional trait are the trunks, little suitcases, and numerous other charming accessories that accompany Jody's bears. *Photograph by Jeff Battaglia.*

11. *Susie Gumdrop.* 1995. 7in (18cm); stressed (for vintage look) synthetic plush; black glass eyes; fully jointed; excelsior stuffing. Fetchingly outfitted in a periwinkle linen dress, a white velveteen hat. Carries a cherry lollipop.

10

Wendy Brent

Before bears were my art dolls. Then, 15 years ago, my bears came along with the head in a rose petal effect and the body and hands out of fur. At first I made the bears with cinnamon snouts; some had nutmeg snouts and I went wild with these! Then, came the "Tibetan bears," with gorgeous long fur.

Now, I'm quite happy making my bears out of a new pattern I create in curly mohair. Their paws are specially made in mostly darker colors. The eyes are quite special. They are ordered from Germany with no coloring on the bottom, only black in the center. I make them blue, sometimes green, sometimes lavender, sometimes gold. They are very plain as they start and then they get so lovely as I sit and work with them and fire them in the kiln.

I do three Teddy Bear shows a year. Most people who buy my bears spend between $125 to $350. My bears also go to the New York Toy Fair, Los Angeles Show, and the Atlanta Show. These shows are special because they sell wholesale only to people who buy my bears, rabbits, and cats for their stores.

12. Wendy Brent has focused on art since she was a child. She became fascinated by the utilitarian aspects of sculpture and began creating dolls. The Teddy Bears she first designed in 1983 have proven to be the most loved of all her creations.

13. *Lord Bluestone.* 1995. 22in (56cm) tall and made of curly mohair.

11

Deanna Brittsan
BEARS BY DEANNA BRITTSAN

14. Deanna Brittsan has won many awards for the bear designs she has produced since the early 1980s.

I've been making bears since 1982 when I found a bear pattern in a doll magazine. Today I am best known for old, aged-looking bears, especially my Santa Claus bear. I'm also known for my great props and bear decorating in any room and for all occasions.

I make about 100 to 350 bears a year and do about four shows. I have made up to 75 of the same bear, but usually stop at 25 or 30. All my bears have sewn-in cloth or leather tags with the date on them (for the antique looking bears).

Prices range from $85 for the 8in (20cm) bears up to $350 for the 22in (56cm). I prefer to make mid-size bears as my arthritis is getting bad and the larger ones are too difficult for me to make. All are usually out of mohair with the fur aged by me. I also like to dye my own fur.

The most unique bear making experience turned out to be trying to keep my first head from wobbling. I was experimenting with cardboard discs, cutting and gluing them together to make a strong disc, but when I used the small ones, I was making for arms and legs, the head never stayed up straight. I couldn't figure out what was wrong. Finally, my daughter Debbie said, "Mom, why don't you make it bigger around?" It worked!

15. *Buckles.* 1993. 13in (33cm). Each bear is fully jointed, made of different colors of mohair with shoe button eyes. Old buckles are used on each bear's outfit.

12

Jean Burhans
CRITTERS

16. It took considerable persuasion for friends and family to convince Jean Burhans that her "Critters" would be accepted at bear shows among the traditional bears. However she gained confidence when she almost sold out at the "Teddy Bear Reunion In The Heartland" in 1995. *Photograph by Woodside Photography.*

All of my bears have soft-sculptured faces which allows for many different expressions. Some are over-stuffed with soft-sculptured bellies. Many are busy doing something, but I do create several "Critters" just for cuddling.

In 1985, after I saw a simply-made bear in a magazine, I decided to make Teddy Bears for all the family as gifts. I used a cotton ribbed knit for the faces. They were quite primitive looking, but my own design at least, and quite well received.

Two people are very important to my production of between 200 to 250 bears a year. The first is my husband, Paul, who makes all the armatures for any size bear. He also creates many props. Another lady sews the bodies for me. I cut-out, stuff, make all the heads, and clothes.

My bears are predominantly one of a kind. I may repeat them, but never exactly the same bear. I have, on occasion, done a limited edition, but faces are never identical. The largest bears I make are 36in (91cm), for $200 and the smallest 8in (20cm), for $95. People usually respond to my work with smiles, giggles, and an occasional belly laugh.

17. *The Family Stroll.* 1995. (Left to right) *Mama.* 18in (46cm); *Baby Bear* (in stroller) 6in (15cm). *Big Brother* (hanging on stroller) 9in (23cm). *Papa.* 19in (48cm). All bears have posable armature encased within their unjointed soft plush bodies. Their heads swivel to allow posing for their winsome hand sculpted faces. Their acrylic eyes sparkle with character and love. *Photograph by Woodside Photography.*

Renee & Jim Casey
RENEE'S BEARS & OTHER THINGS

I had been collecting Teddy Bears for about 20 years. Teddies had brought so much joy into my life that I wanted to create and sell small bears to bring joy into the lives of others. I worked on patterns to develop my bears for about a year and a half until I was happy with the designs. In 1991, I began doing bear shows and selling to some stores.

Two years later my husband, Jim, was laid off. We were not sure what we were going to do next. After 30 years in the aerospace industry, Jim rediscovered his love of woodworking. Joan Woessner, a Teddy Bear artist, encouraged Jim to make a small sewing machine cabinet similar to one she had but that was no longer available. Jim designed and built a prototype and we started getting orders right away. The first two orders were from collectors who did not have antique toy machines, but wanted us to find them for their cabinets. The search was on. While we were looking everywhere for toy sewing machines, we found antique sewing accessories.

We were getting to know each other again after 23 years of marriage. His love of woodworking, my love of Teddy Bears, and the our mutual interest in antiques blended together wonderfully. We do shows together and our business is growing.

I make a lot of different miniature bears. My newest design is a miniature Limited Edition teddy called *Victorian Pincushion Teddy* to go with our sewing items. We also have a *Thimble-Head Teddy*.

18. Renee and Jim Casey with a representation of their delightful miniature teddies, quality handmade reproduction miniature sewing cabinets, and antique sewing accessories.

BEAR MAKING HINTS: Remember, if you are going to sell your bears at a show, your display is very important. You want your display to attract people. Once they stop at your display, you are on your way to a sale. This is why we change our display around several times in a year.

19. *Victorian Pin Cushion Teddies.* These two, charming, fully jointed bears are made of soft blue upholstery fabric with black glass bead eyes. Each bear in this edition has a pincushion and no two are alike. Limited edition of 50.

Allen Chau/ Robert Welch
WHATABEAR

20. Allen Chau (left) and Robert Welch (right) found their bears were extremely well received in Japan. Pictured at their booth at the Japan Teddy Bear Association's 1993 convention is one of the young Japanese collectors (Iyori Hirose) who fell in love with one of the artists' larger bear creations.

In 1988, while driving down the Central Coast of California, the thought crossed our minds that since we were both spending so much on bear collecting that maybe we could supplement our bear purchasing power by creating and selling our own bears.

What could we do to make our bears different? As a classroom teacher, Bob often draws whimsical new characters on chalk boards and dittos. One such character is Bruno, the concept for our bears, a bear with a smiling face.

Using a sewing machine was nothing new to Bob who had made and costumed puppets he used in his shows as a professional puppeteer. When the first bear, *Algy*, was completed to our satisfaction, I put one of my bow ties on the bear and thus came about our signature of a handmade, hand-tied bow tie that appears on our logo bear.

Next came naming our bears. Haven't we all at sometime or other said, "What a great looking bear!" Or "What a cute bear!" Or "What a bear!" So we came upon the name "Whatabear."

From our first bear, *Algy,* to our most recent designs, Bob and I have tried to make our designs interesting, different, and lovable. All of our bears are fully jointed and have either glass or shoe button eyes. All are made from mohair, alpaca, morino wool, or imported synthetics. We produce approximately 150 bears a year that are particularly identifiable by the "Whatabear" look of cheeks and a smile. Whatabears range in size from 8—23in (28—58cm) tall and sell for $45 to $300.

21. The enchanting smiling faces of Robert Welch and Allen Chau's bear creations have stolen the hearts of collectors around the world. They are made in limited and open end editions.

15

Sue Coe
BEAR FEET

My aunt, Shirley Gibbard, taught me how to make bears. My mother taught me to sew when I was ten, and I've been sewing ever since. I worked as an alteration person for a large department store for five years. I made a go of Teddy Bear making in 1982 and haven't hemmed a pair of pants since.

It was when I had an operation on my left leg that I started making bears for sale. Even today, the white tag sewn in the left leg of all my bears is a symbol of that time. Each tag says Bear Feet, 148 Fowler Dr., Monrovia, CA 91016, (818)358-2029 in red.

My bears are sold both retail and wholesale. I specialize in weighted undressed mohair bears. The smallest, *Schotzi* is 6in (15cm) tall, weighs two pounds and sells for $55! The largest, *Brittney,* is 25in (64cm) with a yes/no mechanism and sells for $275.

My only helper is my husband Roger. He draws my patterns on the fur and helps with jointing.

Last year, I made a little more than 400 Teddy Bears. I do 11 shows a year from close to home to Tokyo and Glasgow. I teach workshops at Conventions. Most of my bears are open ended but I have done three Limited Editions. I have over 15 different patterns that I use.

The most difficult part of bear making is marketing. Although I have become less shy and more self-confident over the years, it is still hard to get your name out and advertising is so expensive. I want to give my customers the most for their money and when you have to add in advertising costs to a bear, it makes the bear out of reach to many people.

It took me almost nine years before the first person came up to me and said "Oh, I know your bears!" I am glad that I never gave up.

BEAR MAKING HINTS: Use a french knot when cloing your bears. The knot has never failed. The thread has broken, but never the knot. You can find how to do this by looking in any embroidery book.

22. Sue Coe worked hard to reach the recognition in the bear world she possesses today. The highlight of her career was in 1995 when she was invited to be one of the Teddy Bear artists to exhibit her work at Walt Disney World®'s prestigious Teddy Bear and Doll Convention in Florida.

23. *Nikki.* 1994. 7in (18cm); Merino wool and alpaca blend; blown glass black eyes; fully jointed; yes/no mechanism encased in head and body. Each bear in this series wears a different hand-knitted sweater.

Wanda Cole
FOREVER OREGON BEARS

I started making bears privately in 1984. In 1986 I turned professional and started on my first show circuit. Now, I exhibit at 10 to 13 shows per year and produce less than 100 one-of-a-kind bears a year from vintage fur coats, capes, and collars.

My bears are identified by their trademark leather noses, tri-sculptured faces, and bodies of real fur. They've been televised and published in hardback books. They've won ribbons for best of class in various state conventions and in 1996 I have a calendar coming out.

I receive much pleasure from making bears that are highly unusual and difficult. The faces mean a lot to me. I might spend 3-1/2 to 4 hours sculpting the fur and nose, and even more time when I inset several fur pieces. It is exciting to see the spirit radiate throughout the facial features of a new bruin.

I find the hardest task in making my bears is breathing in real fur hair and turning the bear inside out without losing the bear. Because the coats I use are old, and even though I treat the cape back and line the fur, sometimes the bear will blow out due to thin hide or dryness. When all that work is lost, I just want to cry.

My bears vary in price and size due to clothing, insetting multiples of fur, shading, and so on. A typical 8in (20cm) bear goes for $150. Bears 20—29in (51—74cm) can sell for $350 to $450. Show bears and auction pieces begin at $699 and rare fur bears are $650 and higher.

The most pleasure I get from marketing my bears is meeting wonderful collectors from all walks of life. It is particularly gratifying to make a bear from a customer's fur and watch the expression on their face reflecting sentimental tears or happy smiles and hugs when their family heirloom is transformed into special bears.

BEAR MAKING HINTS: In working with real fur...
1. Release the linings on coats to see if the hide is not too dry to make a bear.
2. Always line the fur with high quality cotton.
3. Stay stitch all openings.
4. Cut pattern pieces from cotton, glue to stripped coat (now in yardage form).
5. Use razor blade or furrier knife to cut out the bear fur.
6. Double or triple stitch all bear parts and line paw pads and foot pads.

SALES HINTS:
1. Be professional. Dress up, use breath spray, be friendly, and don't clutter your table.
2. Use a non-distracting tablecloth that drapes to the floor.
3. Use soft mood music and lights with a few good props to enhance your display.
4. Educate potential customers about the industry: the variety of furs, designing, and what a collectible is.

24. Wanda Cole's bears are identified by their trademark leather noses, tri-sculptured appealing faces, and warm bodies of real fur.

25. *Shadow.* 1995. 18in (46cm); crafted from five colors of mink; glass eyes; fully jointed. All of Wanda Cole's bears are one-of-a-kind and are created from fully lined vintage fur coats, capes, and mink collars.

17

Pam Collins-White
THE TOYMAKER

My bear, Ted, was always my favorite toy. I wanted to make my daughter Hillary a bear that would mean as much to her, so I made her Pumpkin. My high school art teacher was fresh out of college and definitely a free thinker. He influenced me to create as I wished.

I began with bears alone. Then I did fabric decoys for several years and eventually branched out to other animals. All of my bears were designed for special people as gifts. I do them out of mohair and velveteen.

In 1992, I was commissioned to design all the animals for Tiffany & Co.'s Easter window display. Then, in 1993 I was invited to create three pieces for a show called "Concerning Humor" at the Barn Gallery in Ogunquit, ME. *Boomer Raccoon, Francis M. Fox,* and *Rudi Rabbit* were a result of that exhibit.

Although they are not all bears, I do produce about 750 animals a year. I love finishing them and looking at their faces. They all have personalities of their own. Some are mischievous and others are innocent. My animals seem to evoke fond memories and people love to share them with me.

26. Pam Collins-White gained some of her experience in working on bears through the many operations she performed on restoring her beloved childhood bear Ted. *Photograph by J. Kevin White.*

27. *Boomer Raccoon and Bing Bear. Boomer.* 1993. 24in (61cm); gray and black (tipped) mohair and alpaca; German glass eyes; fully jointed; hands, fingers, and toes are fully wired. Accessories: fishing pole (not pictured). Limited edition of 150. *Bing Bear.* 1987. 10in (25cm); short gold mohair; German glass eyes; fully jointed. Accessories: hat, scarf and red wooden sled (not pictured). *Photograph by J. Kevin White.*

Anne Cranshaw
E. WILLOUGHBY BEAR COMPANY

I began making Teddy Bears more than ten years ago when my then five year old daughter, Joy, wanted a Teddy Bear muff. Within a couple of months I was making bears for sale.

I am primarily interested in bears with movement and have used a variety of techniques to create bears that can be posed in a variety of ways. These include pellets, Loc-Line® armature, wire and Flex-Limb armatures, removable heads, and bears with nine joints. A few designs are unjointed, made especially for young children.

Most of the 3600 bears I've made over the years are jointed and made of mohair. However, I have also used plush, alpaca, and wool. For the past few years, I have made 250 to 300 bears a year. One year I made 600. Most of the limited editions have been 10—50 bears.

Currently, I have an unjointed 12in (31cm) bear that sells for $35. My mohair bears start at $90 for a 5in (13cm) and go up to $325 for a 24in (64cm) bear. One-of-a-kind bears occasionally sell for more.

I was a grade school teacher, so when I am not making bears, I teach Teddy Bear making to others. This is really fun and satisfies my teaching needs as well as promoting bears.

Some of my bears have had quite unusual features. A series of six English queens were designed with heads that can be unscrewed and held in arms with wire inserts. Each was intricately costumed in styles accurate to the time period.

My awards and prize list continues to grow since my first award in 1987 for "Heroes of the American Tea Party." My bear *John Rowe* represented a colonial ancestor of mine who disguised himself as an Indian, with an Indian costume of leather, glass beads, and feathers over a colonial shirt. My most recent First Prize was for *Anne's Orphan*, the people's choice award at the Maine Society of Doll and Bear Artists in Saco, Maine.

BEAR MAKING HINTS:
1. Have other interests and activities in your life to prevent burn out and provide inspiration.
2. Keep each bear in a zippered plastic bag from the time it is cut out until the final stuffing. By keeping bears in various stages of completion, you can move to a different part of the process if you become tired or bored.
3. If you experience pain in your wrists or arms, STOP. Move on to a different part of the process or rest completely for a while, even a day or two, if necessary.

28. Anne Cranshaw encases the Loc-Line® armature in the arms and legs of her bears giving them immense hugging ability. *Photograph by Gene Willman Photo.*

29. *Ebearneezer Scrooge.* 1992. 18in (46cm); made of light brown silk/alpaca; German glass eyes; fully jointed. Character from Dickens' *A Christmas Carol* has wire armature in arms so he can hold three masks which represent the three ghosts of Christmas. The masks are made from wool felt, painted, and trimmed. They are molded to fit the bear's face. One-of-a-kind.

Rhoda Curtis
REMINDER SHOP

30. For many years Rhoda Curtis of Edmonds, Washington has been an important figure of the Teddy Bear world in the Pacific Northwest. She was an enthusiastic and caring member and patron of the Teddy Bear artists in the early 1980s. She promoted many new artists through her wonderful store, the Reminder Shop. Though Rhoda had to close the store because of ill health, she still is very much valued as an artist in the bear genre creating an increasingly limited number of exquisite small to miniature bears prized for their sweetness, imagination, and rarity.

I truly love making whimsical bears in very small quantities. They all have rosy cheeks and most are 8in (20cm) or under.

Although I have been collecting bears since I was three, I always considered myself a non-sewer. Most of my talent had been in music and I even recorded an album of my own compositions for United Artist Records.

At my shop, a wonderful bear maker named Joan Erdahl offered a class and she needed one more person to fill it. I really resisted, but to my amazement, I came out of the class with a bear I loved making and actually thought was cute!

Until I became ill, I was very active in the Seattle area Teddy Bear world and participated in clubs and taught classes. I was given a "Rhoda Curtis Appreciation Day" by our two local clubs and I was very honored by this expression of generosity and kindness. Now I sometimes give small bear making classes in my home.

My bears are sold in about 12 local bear sales a year (I produce about 100); a friend of mine is kind enough to sell them for me since I can't go myself. They retail from $40 to $150.

I hate pricing bears! I hate selling them! I wish I could give them all away as presents!

31. A representation of the exquisite workmanship of this creative artist. Each of Rhoda's appealing scenes carry a message: If friends were flowers I'd pick you! The bears range in size from 2-5in (5-13cm). Crafted in upholstery fabric, their fully jointed bodies are dressed in handmade outfits of fabric leaves, silk flowers, and antique doily remnants. *Photograph by George Comito.*

20

32. Bears range in size from 4-8in (10cm-20cm). The small bears have jointed and unjointed bodies and are made of upholstery fabric with black glass bead eyes. The two larger bears are fully jointed, made of distressed mohair with black glass eyes. All bears are artistically dressed in a Christmas theme. 1990-1993. *Photograph by George Comito.*

Sandra Dineen
SANDY'S BEARLY BRUINS

The art of making bears is a fun as well as profitable business. I reluctantly took several bear making classes in 1991 and made my first bear out of acrylic fur. My hobby became infectious and I couldn't wait to return home from my job as office manager at a dental office to work on my bears, often staying up until 2-3 a.m. With each bear I made, the pattern changed. I made the arms longer, the snout longer, the hump larger — all to give the bear an earlier look.

In 1992, my friend Harriet, who took lessons with me and also owns a Teddy Bear store, suggested I put several of my bears on consignment. Much to my surprise, a very special bear collector bought 16 of my bears. Then I participated in a show at her store with several of the very best and well-known artists. I was honored but petrified. When I sold four bears, well, that was the beginning.

My husband helps me at shows with set-ups and all the heavy work that is involved. When he is home and I'm running behind with orders, he will help me stuff the arms and legs of the bears. I also have a high school girl who enjoys helping me by turning the bears after the sewing which saves the pain in my arthritic fingers.

33. Sandra Dineen dresses her bears in vintage clothing therefore, the majority of her designs are one-of-a-kind.

I usually exhibit at approximately ten shows a year, showing my 150 bears which are traditional with an antique look. All are made with German or English mohair with German glass eyes and jointed with hardboard discs and nuts and bolts. I enjoy dressing the bears in vintage clothing. They range from 13—23in (33—58cm). They are priced from $150 to $260.

I sell bears retail at shows and through advertising in *Teddy Bear and Friends®* and *Teddy Bear Review.* I also sell wholesale to store owners. Some of my bears, which have received ribbons in artist shows, are a Southwestern bear and an English Peddler Lady.

Over time I have built confidence in myself and my work. For a long time I felt like a rookie instead of a professional. It takes several shows and several advertisements in the magazines before feeling comfortable. After practice, practice, and practice, each bear gets better!

34

Luwana Eldredge
KARE 'N' LOVE BEARS 'FUTURE ANTIQUES'

Two years ago, last Christmas, I created my first bear. It seemed inevitable since I live next door to distinguished bear artist Joan Woessner. She was my whole inspiration, not only are her bears beautiful, but I've never met such a giving and talented person before. No matter how busy Joan gets, she always finds the time to help me, especially before my first shows. To me, Joan is a real example of a true bear artist.

My first bear stood 2in (5cm) high and took two weeks to make. Even though I was hooked, or should I say pawed, my whole life was drastically changed. I was too busy sewing to eat or cook for that matter. Along with me, my family lost a few pounds. My sons, especially Michael (15), are a big part of my bear world and my husband is also extremely supportive.

My bears range from 1—14in (3—36cm). My most popular and most favorite are what I call my Patty Cake Bears and they are 4—4-1/2in (10—11cm) tall. They are complete with dresses, shoes, and panties. I do all my own sewing, but my mom, Ruthie, sews all of my dresses. For fur, I use everything from regular upholstery to mohair. My favorite fur is the Viscose.

I concentrate on my faces a lot. For each bear I make, there are two to three other heads that I decided not to use.

Fabric dying is one of my specialties. I dye everything with Ritz Dye®. I've come up with some beautiful fuschia colors. It's great fun to experiment, but make sure to measure your dyes and make note of what colors you've used.

Top to Bottom: **34.** Luwana Eldredge poses with her biggest fan, her son Michael, who helps with his younger brothers, just so Mom can make bears! The sweet, innocent faces of Luwana Eldredge's diminutive bears have an irresistible appeal. Each bear is made of hand-dyed viscose or silk alpaca and wears a uniquely darling dress with either a bonnet or tiny bow(s) affixed at the ear.

35. *Jester Bears.* 1995. The beautiful muted colors used to create the various designs of Jester bears were achieved by dying the fabrics. Each *Jester* is one-of-a-kind.

35

22

Bearmaking began for me in 1990. As part of recovery therapy, heart patients are required to use something soft and weighted. When my grandmother found herself in this position, I wanted to do something special for her. Since I hadn't used a sewing machine since grade school, I asked my future mother-in-law to help me make an "Open Heart Bear." Not having plastic pellets available, the bear's little belly was filled with dried peas! But to this day he sits in a basket over my grandmother's bed watching over her as he did in the hospital.

Since making and giving that first bear, I have had other family members hospitalized or ill and a bear was always by their side. In advertently, I suppose, I've created my own superstition, for now I'm afraid to keep one.

After learning the mechanics of bear making, I decided I would draw my own pattern. I eventually formed a look that distinguished my bears from other artist bears. They are made from mohair, alpaca, and some vintage/antique fabrics. The majority of them are undressed, though occasionally one may wear an antique dress or bib. Many say that my bears look as though they have cheeks. This is due to the "runway" style shaved face and extra long (1in+/3cm+) mohair pile. My bears are further identified with a label at the back seam and each comes with a "Bearied Treasure" map with a brass reproduction gold doubloon hanging off the neck.

I began designing and making my own bears as a way of supplementing my income. This was not easy. Eventually the bears replaced my original career as a dancer. But my dance training and choreography degrees are surprisingly applicable in utilizing many movement principles to my bears and other creatures.

Collectors can expect to spend between $70 to $700 for one of my creations which range in size from 8—25in (20—64cm).

BEAR MAKING HINTS: Since the bear's identity is also part of its collectability, I have devised a registration method that works well.
1. Each bear has a registration number that I keep. This way if a bear was accidentally damaged or destroyed, the collector could retrieve the tags, read me the registration number, and I could reproduce the bear.
2. Tracking bruins also gives you an accurate record of how many bears you've made in a given year.
3. Numbering can be simple or complicated. For instance, registration #501B18-95-71: the first six digits refer to a bent leg/arm 18in design; 95 represents the year, and 71 denotes the number of bears that year.
4. I also photograph each bear and staple it's picture to the page that lists all the bear's materials, registration number, costs, and date it was made.
5. Duplicate the record keeping should an accident occur on your end.

36. Kimberly Fischer discovered her love of bear making was so great, she made the major decision to change her career from a modern ballet dancer, that she had trained for since childhood, to a full-time bear artist.

37. *Porkchops 'n' Applesauce.* 1995. *Applesauce* (Bear). 23in (58cm); Cream colored curly swirly mohair; black glass eyes; fully jointed; handmade apple-floral wreath; sheer imported ribbon. *Porkchops* (Pig). 1995. 11in (28cm); hand-dyed pink mohair and black wool felt paws; black glass eyes; fully jointed; dried apple collar.

23

38. *Tundra and Peep's Ice Fishing Adventure.* 1994. *Tundra* (Bear.) 25in (64cm); white curly mohair; black glass eyes; fully jointed. Accessorized with mini-snowshoes, tree bark backpack, wool scarf, birch walking stick, ultrasuede airbrushed fish, bamboo fishing pole, and Noah bell. *Peep.* (Penguin). 14in (36cm); alpaca and hand-dyed mohair; black glass eyes; fully jointed; wired wings; wool scarf. Sold as a pair. Limited edition of 20. 1994 Golden Teddy Award winner and 1994 TOBY® nominee.

Robin Foley
RAG-O-MUFFINS

I have several lines of limited editions and produce about ten spectacular, one-of-a-kind pieces a year. I also try to take on three or four commissions for non-bear creatures per year. All in all, I produce about 175 bears a year. To this date, I have made only mohair bears which range in size from 12—42in (31—104cm) and price from $120 to $1200.

In the beginning, I started to make very traditional bears. I moved on to make more realistic bears with claws, leather details, and a whole new line called "Couture Creatures."

After focusing solely on bears, I ventured beyond them. Bunnies were the first step and this seemed to invite special requests for more challenging animals such as koalas, penguins, and foxes. This was the perfect opportunity to begin experimenting with fully articulated armatures.

Recently I have opened the Callisto line of bears. These are fully articulated and dressed in Renaissance inspired clothing. Many of them even have feather wings, but it is the leather nose and eye details that give them their personalities.

Most of my work I sell at shows and mail-order. The rest go to a few select shops as time allows.

My background in textiles and commercial illustration have proved to be valuable in my bear making career. However, when I teach workshops at conventions, my focus is on business related themes.

39. Robin Foley proudly holds her bear creation, *Orion.* This enchanting bear won the West Coast Crystal Artist Bear Award at Linda Mullins' San Diego Teddy Bear Event in 1995. *Photograph by Jamie Bosworth.*

BEAR MAKING HINTS:

1. Start with an idea and explore it thoroughly. Experiment in the extreme; you can always do less. If you don't experiment with the extremes, you may never find that special spark that makes your bear an artist bear.

2. A tip for closing the head: stuff it firmly. Install the joint with the disc and hardware in place. Using a long length of very strong thread (doubled) gather the edge of the neck. Draw it tight and tie it. Then put the needle through about three or four gathers and make another knot. Don't cut the thread. Instead, put the needle through another three or four gathers and make another knot. Continue until you've chained knots all the way around the closure. This will give you an extremely strong and reliable neck seam.

40. *Anna Korrina* 1995. 20in (51cm); light beige distressed mohair; enameled blue glass eyes; sculpted leather nose and eye casing; armature encased throughout body; swivel/tilt neck. Regally dressed in a white silk dress embellished with rhinestones, vintage trims, and fur. Delicate metallic netting attached to hat covers the bear's ears.

41. Each of these 1994 and 1995 designs have a unique and fascinating appeal. *Nakita*, (the large bear) has resin clay claws. *Pierre*, the penguin's beak and feet are made of resin and clay. *Duffy*, the rabbit's head nods "yes" and "no." Some of the animals have armature. All are made of mohair with glass eyes.

Marsha Friesen
FRIENDS FOREVER

42. Marsha Friesen has fun creating her fascinating animal characters. *Goat Billy* is a one-of-a-kind 48in (122cm) puppet, sculpted in foam with fabric covering, long synthetic fur, and a fully jointed body.

I love making bears, especially because I share this love with my two daughters, Kim and Mica. They had been making bears for several months when they asked me to make clothing for their little creations. After seeing the response to their dressed bears, I felt it was time for us to make it a threesome!

At this time, we did not know there was such a thing as an artist bear or there were shows especially for marketing them. It wasn't until we came across our first bear magazine that the full potential of bear making opened up for us. We began attending shows and then started advertising in magazines.

Marketing is still a difficult task being that we live in an isolated area of Southeastern Idaho. The nearest town has a population of 3,600 and the largest is 50,000. Most of the people here have never heard of an artist bear and most of them view a teddy bear as only a toy for children. It has been a long, but rewarding process to teach people about collectible bears made of mohair and fully jointed with glass eyes.

I do all my own work except during the busy season of October through December when I hire someone to cut out bears for me. My husband and son also help stuff during this busy time. I make about 150 to 200 bears a year and most of them are large and dressed. I could perhaps expand the amount of bears I make by hiring a full time cutter and investing in a stuffing machine. But, I like the artist bear concept, with each bear being totally designed and made by me. If I were to expand, I would always keep a line of bears that I make from start to finish.

I believe the sky is the limit in the bear world. At this point I still ponder how much of the sky I want in my life.

BEAR MAKING HINTS:
1. When antiquing mohair or bear clothing use a spray bottle with a fine spray nozzle. A warm brown dye lasts longer and is not as acidic as tea dyes.
2. To get a rectangular nose on straight, use a fade out fabric marker to mark out the nose and mouth before beginning. Use long straight pins to mark the position and size of the nose. Sew over the pins starting at the center of the nose and moving to the outside edge. Then retrace back to the center. Then embroider the other side the same way. This will give you a very even and well-proportioned nose.

43. (Left) *Grandma Hattie.* 1993. 25in (64cm); brown mohair; black glass eyes; fully jointed. She wears adult woman's clothing and vintage eyeglasses. Limited edition of 10. (Right) *Little Mugsy.* 1993. 12in (31cm); pale beige mohair; black glass eyes; fully jointed; loosely stuffed with polyester pellets. Limited edition of 25.

Pat Fye
PAT FYE ORIGINALS

When my daughter wanted a bear back in 1980, she signed me up for a bear making class. That was the start of Pat Fye Originals. Eleven years later I won the Golden Teddy Award.

Perhaps the most exciting thing that ever happened to me was in 1984. I designed a *Jack-in-the-Box* bear and took it to the L.A. Beckman Show, a gift show for handmade items. The president of Enesco® Corporation was there looking for new ideas, as he often does. He saw the *Jack-in-the-Box* bear and asked about the artist. He got my phone number and called that night, offering me a five year contract with Enesco® to design a Christmas series of them and other things in the future. It took me a good three months to come down to earth.

Now I produce 350 to 400 bears ranging from 3–14in (8–61cm) and priced from $100 to $400. I also make a bear which stands on all-fours which measures 7in x 10in (18cm x 25cm).

44. Pat Fye believes in striving for quality. Creating her own special look and staying with it works best for her in fabricating her bears.

45. A wonderful array of Pat Fye's unique Rolly Polly bears. Produced in 1993 each piece is 2-1/2in (6cm) tall, made of upholstery fabric with glass bead eyes. The base is weighted to bounce the bear back when rolled over.

Barbara Garrett
BG BEARS

46. Barbara Garrett is renowned for producing exquisite costumed miniature bears artistically displayed in adorable intricate scenes. Pictured is *Mama Bear's House*. Barbara found an antique shoe perfect for creating a little house for her tiny teddies.

I have been collecting dolls for most of my life. In order to finish off one of my doll scenes, I wanted to have a doll holding a miniature bear, but couldn't find one anywhere. From looking at larger bears, I made a small one, using some ultrasuede I had. From that point, I started making more for other dolls and other friends. Several months passed before I realized the potential for bear making. In the summer of 1991, I began making bears for a local shop.

My bears are generally designed to look like well-known storyland, fictional, and historical figures. The sizes range from 5/8—4-1/2in (2—12cm).

I try to produce one to three bears every working day. Dressed bears usually take a full day each and there are both limited editions and open-ended series. The price range of each bear depends on the amount of work involved. For instance, my *Captain Hook* is 4-1/4in (10.65cm), takes six hours or more to make properly, costing $140. Dressed bears alone range from $95 to $140. Shoes (*Old Lady in the Shoe*) range from $350 to $615, depending on the number of bears purchased with the shoe. All my bears have a small circular plastic tag on them, bearing the initials "BG."

I do design and generally make the bears myself, with some help cutting patterns by family members. I recruit help among my sisters and children for on the road shows. My goal is to do no more than two shows a month. It is hard to keep up with road shows, find time to produce quality and the number of bears needed, and to come up with new designs for my growing number of established customers.

47. *Peter Pan, Hook, Tinkerbell, Wendy, Michael, John.* 1994. 1-1/2—4-1/2in (4—12cm); acrylic bodies with ultrasuede paw and foot pads; glass eyes; fully jointed. Fully costumed in ultrasuede, nylon, cotton, and terry cloth. Limited edition of 10 sets.

48. *Geppetto & Pinocchio* (Puppet & Puppetmaster). 1994. 3in (8cm); acrylic bodies with ultrasuede paw and foot pads; glass eyes; fully jointed. Fully costumed in ultrasuede; wooden props; pencil and ruler.

Mary George
MARY GEORGE BEARS

Believe it or not it was Linda Mullins' first book, *Teddy Bears Past and Present (Vol. I)* which inspired me to make bears. I came across it in the library while researching antiques and early American decor when my husband and I were redecorating certain rooms in our home. When I saw the Teddy Bear faces in the book, it was "love at first sight." In 1987, about nine months after I made my first jointed bear, I began selling antique-style Teddy Bears.

My teddies have won a Best of Show ribbon in two Teddy Bear contests. One of my bears was a 1994 TOBY® nominee.

I sell my Teddy Bears directly to collectors through mail order and at Teddy Bear shows (only 3 to 4 a year). I find it is hard to sell through the mail. I like to think of each bear as an individual and I have a difficult time getting any kind of catalog put together. I tend to get very bored using the same mohair over and over or making the same basic kind of bear again and again. Also, since I make one bear at a time, I like to vary the size, color, and style with each bear. I frequently make changes in the bear's design as I trace my patterns on the mohair, just to see what I'll get. I am still trying to figure out how to let collectors know what kind of bears I make without getting tied down to making the same bears time after time.

I have made bears as small as 4—5in (10—13cm) and as large as 32in (81cm), but my usual range of sizes is 10—27in (25—69cm). My prices can vary from $90 to $450, depending on the size of the bear and the mohair used.

My son has a chronic medical problem that can require hospitalization or a lot of medical care at home at times. I try to make two to three bears per week when things are going well, but this could suddenly change to two or three bears a month if things become serious with my son's health.

My goal is to make each teddy look like he's alive and ready to talk to you.

BEAR MAKING HINTS: When selecting a pair of eyes to place in a bear's face, cut out 3in x 5in (8cm x 13cm) pieces of mohair in a variety of lengths and glue them on 3in x 5in (8cm x 13cm) cards. Then punch two holes about 1in (3cm) apart. Place a glass eye in each hole to see if the eyes are a good match. Since glass eyes can be so inconsistent in their size and shape, this helps choose eyes that match with more ease and accuracy than holding them up in the air and comparing.

49. Mary George makes antique-style Teddy Bears. She loves the features found in the bears of the early 1900s and strives to incorporate them into her bears.

50. *Old German Bears.* 1995. (Left) 20in (51cm); blonde, curly distressed mohair. (Right) 23in (58cm); chocolate brown curly distressed mohair. Both bears have black glass eyes are fully jointed and have center-seamed heads.

29

Barbara Golden
CAN'T BEAR TO PART

51. Barbara Golden demonstrates the huggable appeal of bear creation *Bruin*. Limited edition of 250. *Photograph by Shawn Green.*

I was an international banker in Europe and a corporate banker in New York City. I have an M.B.A. in international finance. However, when I went to my first bear show in Florida in 1991, I was immediately captivated by the work I saw, especially that of the Paisley Bears. By the next year, I was making bears for sale.

Since bear making is my only livelihood, it is run as a serious business. I constantly need to balance creative energy with financial realities. I must live with compromise, finding the best design that can be made in the shortest time, at the lowest price.

As wholesale volume is the key to success. I make 400 bears a year, participating in two to three trade shows annually (primarily the International Toy Fair in New York City in February).

Unfortunately, production is the hardest part of running the business. Finding and training part-time sewers is a monumental task. Yet, quite frankly, I remain the real bottleneck. I do all the head and finishing work. Therefore, I can only produce a very limited number of bears each day. I tend to work seven days a week, often averaging 10—12 hours per day. It is a grueling schedule and I am constantly behind on orders.

My bears, limited editions of 50 to 250, have an innovative look that requires some risk in purchase. I work in mohairs, alpacas, and wools with prices ranging from $150 to $420. While maintaining my artist line, I do want to produce a manufactured line at lower prices. I also want to license my designs in a number of product categories.

I have recently won two TOBY® Awards: 1994, for *Alphabear "R"*, Medium Undressed Artist Category and 1995, for *Tweedledee/Tweedledum*, Large Dressed Artist Category.

I enjoy being able to focus on the creative side of my personality, to work with my hands, to maintain a flexible life style, and to make people smile. On the other hand, I appreciate the market place. I listen, watch, and absorb. Good information and a healthy cash flow are as important to me as creativity.

BEAR MAKING HINTS: To make a bear stand on its own: When sewing foot pad to leg, stitch over a piece of paper. Carefully pull out the paper oval that has been created by the stitch line. On hard cardboard, trace 1/8in (.3cm) within first oval. This smaller oval will be cut out and inserted inside leg. Pin the cardboard oval in place like the inner sole of a shoe. (Pins are inserted from the outside). Stuff the leg firmly and remove pins.

TWEEDLEDUM   TWEEDLEDEE

52. *Tweedledee and Tweedledum.* 1995. 16in (14cm); light golden mohair tipped with black; glass eyes; fully jointed; free standing. Part of Barbara's Alice In Wonderland Series. 1995 TOBY® nominee (Large Dressed Artist Bear category). Limited edition of 150 each. *Photograph by Shawn Green.*

30

Barbara Golden
CAN'T BEAR TO PART

53. *The Mad Hatter.* 1995. 14in (36cm); pale gold distressed mohair; glass eyes; fully jointed; self standing; hand sculptured snout with teeth and freckles. Limited edition of 150. Part of Barbara's Alice in Wonderland Series. *Photograph by Shawn Green.*

Frances Harper
APPLE OF MY EYE

54. Frances Harper is surrounded by her regal looking big bruin creations. This is one of Frances' favorite toy corners in her home.

I love making something out of nothing. Whether it be floral design (cutting my own flowers from the garden and arranging them) or refinishing a piece of furniture that has been discarded, or taking a yard of fabric and making a three dimensional creation, the excitement comes when the object lives and you know that you did it yourself.

This was my reasoning when I quit my job as a floral designer after 18 years. I wanted the freedom of working for myself, at what, I didn't yet know. I always loved sewing and at the time the Teddy Bear craze had hit the antique market. Loving the old bears, but not being able to afford to buy them, I tried making one, then another, then another...

Now I make about 375 "Old Timey" bears a year. I attend 15 shows a year, sometimes 17. But, honestly, I would like to cut that number down. My dressed bears are one-of-a-kind, but I produce many that are not dressed and therefore open-ended. All of my larger bears have an "apple of my eye" woven label sewn into the back seam. The smaller ones (6in/15cm) have a printed label. My bears are priced according to size. For instance, the 4-1/2in (11cm) begin at $55. The 30in (76cm) are $390. I make seven sizes in between.

The future is bringing me more and more to the European market. I have been selling in England and Holland for four years. I am participating in the 1995 Artist for Artist European Tour and I would like to expand my market into Germany.

I feel that bears should only go home with someone who truly loves them. Consequently, my bears sell themselves.

BEAR MAKING HINTS:
1. Have a work schedule. With a calendar in front of you, you will be aware of what has to be done in the months ahead. This is also handy in ordering mohair and other supplies.
2. Eliminate paper work by taking a computer course. All your retail and wholesale correspondence, mailing lists, and advertising can be at the touch of a button.

55. (Left) *Nicky.* 1995. 12in (31cm). (Right) *Nicoletta.* 1995. 19in (48cm). Both bears are fully jointed, made of mohair, excelsior stuffed, and have shoe-button eyes.

31

Terry Hayes
PENDLETON'S TEDDY BEARS

56. Terry Hayes feels her production increases considerably when she prioritizes her weekly schedule by which bears need to be made.

I began making bears about 11 years ago. At first I retailed my bears in craft shows; then moved to bear shows, and today I sell retail at shows and through ads, and wholesale, not using a "Rep." Recently I employed a person to cut out bears and sew certain parts to help with the production.

I usually create undressed bears for lack of time to make the costumes. I consider my bears on the cute side, rather than old-fashioned or antique type.

My production is quite high, about 30-35 bears a week working seven days, 12-15 hours a day. I do take off two weeks a year so I make approximately 1500 bears a year. These are usually open edition bears, with some one-of-a-kind bears for auction and customers. I do Christmas Limited Editions every year and exclusives for some shops.

I have been in the *Teddy Bear Artists Annual*, The Michauds *Contemporary Teddy Bear Price Guide*, on the cover of January/February 1995 issue of the *Teddy Bear Review*, and have also won various awards for Teddy Bears at shows. I have given a few seminars at shows from making miniature bears to creating five bears a days, in which I give tips on increasing productivity without losing quality. I have recently cut way back on shows because of the volume I do with wholesale and retail orders. This year I am doing 12 shows, opposed to the 24 shows I use to do.

57. *Scrappy.* 1995. 9in (23cm); scraps of hand-dyed curly mohair; ultra suede paw pads; German glass eyes; fully jointed. All bears in *Scrappy* series are one-of-a-kind.

BEAR MAKING HINTS:

1. Organize your week and then discipline yourself to complete the work each day; then you can accomplish your goal in the number of bears you need to make.
2. Produce on a production line instead of completing one bear at a time.
—Trace all bears for the day.
—Cut all the pieces and arrange them in stacks of legs, arms, etc.
—Cut the paw pads for all the bears.
—Sew all the pieces in one category (e.g., all arms, all legs).
—After all pieces are sewn, comb the fur from the seams to the insides of the bear parts.
—Turn all pieces and place the discs for jointing.
—Joint arms and legs to bodies.
—Stuff all heads and do finish trimming on the faces.
3. Use a dryer sheet while cleaning the excess after cutting. It helps it from sticking to you.
4. Work on the heads before you attach them to the body. It makes it easier.
5. The three-stitch ear made from a circle saves a lot of time when matching both ears on the head. Use a full circle for the ear instead of two separate pieces. Fold the ear and stitch around the arc. Place a small slit in the bottom for turning. After the ear is turned, with fur going up in front, place the needle with a long double strength cord through the slit and out the corner of the ear. Place the needle in the head at the top of where you want the ear to be on the head and bring the needle out of the bottom of where the ear will be placed. Now, secure this with a stitch. Next, bring the needle in at the bottom of the ear and out of the back of the middle of the ear. Secure this with a stitch. Now, bring the needle in the back and out the front of the middle. Secure this with a stitch. (With larger bears, put a few more stitches in the ear to secure it more securely to the head.)
6. Not using pins while sewing saves time, but requires the ability to push and pull so there are no gaps when sewing.
7. Discipline is the biggest factor to a productive day.

Claire Herz
CAPRICIOUS CREATURES

Textiles have always held a great appeal for me. This, coupled with my love for Steiff toys naturally led me to bears. In 1985, while working on 57th St., in New York, a strange set of coincidences sent me into the nearby Bretano's book store, where I found a book by Ted Menten. The very same day, I proceeded down the street to Jerry Brown Fabrics and Paron Fabrics, where I found three bolts of llama plush at $5.00 per yard. I quit my job within a week, bought a car, and have made bears ever since.

In ten years of designing bears, I have made a wide variety in many variations. They range in size from 3—30in (8—76cm), although these outer parameters are extremely rare.

I use to make between 30 to 45 bears a week, then took every fourth week off. Now that I am married with a toddler, I make about 500 pieces a year (about 60% of these are bears). I attend 7 to 10 shows a year and address both a retail and wholesale market. I maintain that an average person with some money to spend should be able to buy a nice, handmade, mohair bear for under $100. (That's what I could afford on a semi-annual basis). For really special pieces, the price ranges from $250 to $500. Sets average about $1200.

I tend to work in series. Now, I pattern everything. Make one, consider possibilities, and decide from there. My favorite edition number is 12. There are two prototypes, to test color and eye placement. One generally goes to the buyer of the edition; the other to charity. Presently I am making one of everything for myself. As of this year, no more than 100 pieces will ever be made of any one thing.

Early pieces say "Wee Bears," with a black tag. Pieces from 1987 say "Wee Dolls." I finally settled on "Capricious Creatures," as that covered all bases. I always felt that signing the critter ruined it, but sometimes I do sign the foot, or the tail, if there is one, or a shaved spot inside the ear.

I have a gifted artist, Agnes Vandenberg (my mother), working with me as a "cutter". My husband, Matt, likes to be in charge of "quality control."

One of my greatest privileges has been to contribute bears to Good Bears of the World, Ronald McDonald House and our local AIDS task force which serves several New Jersey communities.

BEAR MAKING HINTS: Use Marvy Marker Dye Pens® to tone small areas of fur instead of an airbrush. They come in all colors, are color fast, and you can achieve great effects by blending layers of color. (They are also much quieter than airbrushes).

Top to Bottom: **58.** Claire Herz with her unique character doll *The Hatmaker* (left). This excellent piece of artwork is 9in (23cm) tall, made of short ivory mohair with long white mohair accents (hair), and blown glass "googly" eyes. Costumed in felt with upholstery fabric shoes. Removing the hat discloses a "cake" made of ribbons. Pictured on the right is *Grizz.*
59. (Left) *Nokeo* 13in (33cm); dense gold mohair; contrasting mohair feet and hair; white felt hands; fully jointed; glass eyes; German wool felt costume. Prototype for an edition of 12. (Right) *Hicoray.* 6in (15cm); ultra sparse gold mohair; fully jointed; glass eyes. Note the appeal and character the hand-embroidered eyebrows give both of these pieces.

33

Beth Diane Hogan
SOME BEARS AND OTHER BEASTS

I began making Fimo® bear pins in 1982. That inspired me to try bear figures in Fimo®, which drew a lot of attention. One day, I decided to try to use some mohair fabric in creating a stuffed bear. I was so pleased with the result, I began making small stuffed bears.

I now create miniature bears from 1-1/2—2-1/2in (2—9cm). They have all the complete detail of larger bears being completely cotter pin jointed and made from alpaca, mohair, and upholstery fabric. Many are dressed as sailors, jesters, bellhops, pumpkins, bunnies, and children with removable shoes and other tiny accessories. My small plain bears average $85, chubby or bent-leg bears, $95, and fancier bears go up to $200.

I make all of my 150 bears per year. My husband makes wheels or rockers for the bears on all fours. Most of the time my bears are one-of-a-kind; even if I use the same idea over again it is usually in different colors and accessories.

60. Originally entering the bear world with her adorable Fimo® figurines, Beth Hogan decided to try her hand at making a stuffed bear from some mohair fabric from an old couch. She was so pleased with the results she began making small plush bears.

61. (Left) *Old Heartbeat.* 1994. 2in (5cm); coffee dyed upholstery fabric; ultra suede paw pads; seed bead eyes; fully jointed; wobble head. (Center) *Leopard.* 1995. 2in (5cm); upholstery fabric body; ultra suede paw pads; seed bead eyes; fully jointed. (Right) *Fred.* 1995. 3in (8cm); hand-dyed brown upholstery fabric body; ultra suede paw pads; seed bead eyes; fully jointed.

62. Susan Horn's bears are fashioned after antique bear designs, but with softer and usually more feminine allure. She uses many vintage items to costume and accessorize her bears.

63. *Natalie and Naughty* (the puppy). 1994. Bear 16in (41cm); medium brown mohair; glass eyes; fully jointed. *Natalie* carries a muff made of vintage mohair. Her clothing is completely made with vintage items. Her mohair puppy has a jointed neck and antique shoe-button eyes. *Photograph by Gary Mathis.*

I'm still working on designing the "perfect" pattern. I do have a number of basic bear patterns I use, but I don't limit the amount that can be made from any one pattern. I've developed some very sweet faces, which I've gradually changed and perfected over the 3-1/2 years I've been creating bears. Even in repeating a bear such as my "Gardening Girls," so many unique vintage flowers, trims, and accessories are used that they aren't really identical or a true edition.

My bears are influenced by the look of antique bears, but are softer and usually more feminine. I have made bears as large as 26in (66cm) and as small as 4-3/4in (12cm), but I usually concentrate on 10—18in (25—46cm). I've also made many different creatures as companions to my bears; i.e., cats, kittens, dogs, pigs, elephants, chickens, bunnies, baby chicks, frogs, and even a caterpillar.

My latest venture is the design of an exclusive line of collector Teddy Bears for a new division of the Franklin Mint. I'm very excited about it!

35

Debbie Kesling
BEARS BY DEBBIE KESLING

64. Debbie Kesling makes miniature bears 2in (5cm) and under. These well-proportioned teddies are accurately scaled down reproductions of their large counterparts.

65. *Clown Purse Necklace.* 1994. 2-1/2in (6cm); white upholstery fabric; pink ultra suede paw pads; German glass eyes; unjointed; silk thread embroidered face.

I am one of the first Teddy Bear artists to venture into cyberspace (the computerworld of the Internet). My work is featured on a Worldwide Web site in Germany. I also love conducting Teddy Bear business via the Net as it is nearly instantaneous.

I create miniature bears, 2in (5cm) and under, for discriminating collectors. These teddies are well-proportioned, accurately scaled-down reproductions of their large counterparts. They range in price from $170 for a simple, 2in (5cm) teddy, to $1200+ for a one-of-a-kind, multi-bear set made to a client's specifications.

I very much enjoy sharing my bear making techniques with others, which has led me to teach a few classes over the years. I developed a kit for a 2in (5cm) bear which is sold by Good Bears of the World. In 1994, I released my professionally produced videotape and kit set, "Secrets of Miniature Bear Artistry," which has worldwide distribution. It is even available in a Japanese dubbed version.

I typically prefer to sell retail, as a big part of the enjoyment I get from my work is the interaction with my clients. 1995 saw the first mass-production of one of my designs by the Akira Trading Company.

The hardest part of bear making for me is starting a new design from scratch. I sometimes have difficultly with visualizing in three dimensions. I get frustrated very easily and it is not unusual for it to take me 18 months (and many failed attempts) to perfect a new design concept.

BEAR MAKING HINTS:
1. Create a teddy that people will recognize as your work even without an ID tag.
2. Always cut your miniature bear pattern pieces as carefully as you can. With full-size bears, you have some margin for error. With minis, every mistake is amplified.
3. When using glass eyes on wires (for minis), anchor them inside the head with a small plastic disk. Just poke two holes in the disk: one for each eye wire. Snip the long ends off, then snug the wires down with a twist of your hemostats or tweezers.
4. When you finally come up with a miniature bear design that you really like, you can trim quite a few minutes from your making time by having a rubber stamp made.
5. Always wash your fabrics before using them. I like to wash them in hot water with a liquid fabric softener. You can just toss them in the dryer and this sort of "plumps up" the fibers and can add a lot of personality to your bears.
6. Take as long to trim a 2in (5cm) bear's face as a 20in(51cm) bear's face. Snip one hair at a time and you can be fairly certain you won't over trim.
7. For eyes on very small bears, try using jewelry headpins and automotive paint. Take a block of Fimo® or Sculpey® and poke a lot of holes in it with a headpin. Wiggle the pin a bit to enlarge the hole slightly. Dip the head end of each headpin in the paint, then insert in one of the holes you made in the block of clay. When you have inserted all the dipped headpins in the clay, bake very slowly (about 250), until the paint hardens. Remove from oven, then repeat the process. Use your completed eyes as you would glass eyes on wires. These eyes can be somewhat fragile, but used carefully, they will serve you well.

36

Debbie Kesling
BEARS BY DEBBIE KESLING

66. Debbie Kesling's adorable tiny teddy creations promote the artist's video ("Secrets of Miniature Bear Artistry") by enticingly surrounding the tape.

Barbara King
BARBARA KING BEARS

67. Barbara King produces numerous different designs, however, she makes sure each face has the sweet "perky" expression that beguiles the collectors to continue to add her bears to their collections.

From the time I was old enough to use a needle and thread, I sewed clothes for dolls, myself, and my grandchildren. Then I got into making all sorts of crafts and quilting items that I sold at boutiques. Bear making came along on January 30, 1987 when I enrolled in a class on how to make a jointed bear. Since that time, hardly a day goes by that I am not marking, cutting, pinning, sewing, or stuffing a bear.

Not long after my class, I began to develop my own patterns. My bears are best known for their sweet, pouty faces. They range from 9—27in (23—66cm).

Finding supplies was very hard until I heard about a bear show. There I found all I needed and also a bear club. The mohair I purchased that day was a treat since it didn't stretch or distort as the other fabrics did. Since that time, mohair has been my fabric of choice.

My bears have won a variety of awards and have been featured in magazines and books. I felt very honored to be invited as an artist to the First Teddy Bear Classic at Disneyland in 1992.

Recently I have had the pleasure of designing bears for the Annette Funicello Teddy Bear Co. I have also designed a bear for the L.L. Knickerbocker Co. that is a replica of one of the original Knickerbocker Toy Co. bears.

BEAR MAKING HINTS:
1. Make golf size balls with stuffing; then insert one at a time into all sections of the bear, packing firmly with a stuffing tool as you go (from Ted Menten).
2. Trim the nose area to the backing. Place strips of cellophane tape along each side of nose to hold fur out of the way (from Karen Rundlett).

37

The first bear I ever made was from a commercial pattern from Paddington Bear. I made nine of them for Christmas presents, 18 years ago. Three years ago I designed my own pattern for a miniature bear after reading an issue of *Teddy Bear and Friends®* on a long car trip.

I used to do Indian bead work and the men in my family are active black powder shooters. They dress in buckskin and attend rendezvous where most of the people live for the weekend as mountain men. That was my inspiration for making my bears out of deerskin.

Bearskins, The Original Deerskin Bear, consist of 19 pieces or more and have

68. Working in deerskin, Kathy LacQuay's bears consist of 19 pieces or more, which are hand-sewn on the outside. Kathy works alone as the characteristics of the leather make it necessary for her to do the pattern layout, cutting, and stitching herself.

glass bead eyes, an embroidered nose, mouth, and claws. They are fully jointed. They currently retail for $70 to $160 and range in size from 1—3in (2—8cm).

I work alone because the characteristics of the leather make it necessary for me to do the pattern layout, cutting, and stitching myself. The deer hide stretches in different directions at different places on the hide and I am the only one who would be able to tell if that particular spot had too much stretch or not enough to produce a nice bear and be consistent. I have a special way of cutting and preparing the leather to make the seams as invisible as possible. It takes me about six hours to make a bear and two to three hours more for the costume depending on whether or not it is beaded leather or machine sewn. I do a lot of search on costuming before I do an Indian bear and love to work with feathers and beads.

I got into selling bears by writing to several shops around the country and sending pictures, prices, a purchase order, and a letter of introduction. When I didn't hear from the first ten, I sent out ten more. I also looked for shops that would advertise my name and possibly use a picture. The advantage to wholesaling is that it can be done with a minimal amount of designs and you don't have to outlay cash for shows. It wasn't until after I had been wholesaling for a while that I started doing shows. (Now I make between 60-70 bears a year and attend 9-10 shows).

BEAR MAKING HINTS:
1. An all polyester thread works best for stitching through leather. The cotton wrapping on ordinary thread tends to shred about half way through a seam.
2. A triple knot works best at the end of your stitching. Go through your loop three times then pull it tight.
3. Sink your knots by putting the needle back into the seam between the threads and out the other side, pulling the knot inside and sinking it into the stuffing; then clip the thread close to the bear where the needle has exited.

69. (Left) *Running Bear.* 1992. 2-3/4in (7cm); gold deerskin body; black glass bead eyes; fully jointed. Wearing a handmade beaded deerskin coat and a headdress of parakeet feathers with bead accents. Limited edition of 20. (Right) *Little White Dove.* 1994. 2-3/4in (7cm); tan deerskin body; black glass bead eyes; fully jointed. Wearing a handmade beaded white deerskin dress and "moccasins." Limited edition of 20.

Denzil Laurence
PERSONALIZED THEME TEDDY BEARS BY DENZIL

I make one-of-a-kind, often personalized, Teddy Bears. In fact, my first bear was a surprise gift for a friends' wedding. A current woman's magazine had a Teddy Bear pattern and I followed it. My bear was dressed as a biker in a leather jacket with sunglasses. The theme was particularly appropriate as the couple planned to depart on a motorcycle for their honeymoon.

The Teddy Bear was a real hit and requests for other individually costumed bears soon had me quite busy. I've continued to make a "bad biker bear." Now I also make a model motorcycle for the bear to sit on. My most popular bear is the *Phantom of the Opera*. As of March 1995 I have made 65 of these.

I also work from photos and like to be extremely accurate, detailed, and recognizable as miniaturization will allow.

Most of my bears are approximately 12—14in (31—36cm). However, I do make different sizes from 5—17in (13—69cm). My least expensive bear is $80 and my most expensive is $175. Made of the finest quality mohair, alpaca, and imported German synthetics milled specially for Teddy Bears, each bear is fully jointed at head, arms, and legs. This enables the bear to be posed. For example, the tennis player can have a racquet in the air or a baseball player can fling a bat over his shoulder.

You can tell my bears by a similar, delightful facial expression, detailed costuming, and unique props. The ears are lower at the side of the head than many and I always employ a leather nose.

Perhaps the most poignant story I can tell about a personalized bear is one about *Saffron*, who traveled with me to my native New Zealand, during one of my most stressful times. Prior to my journey home, in 1993, I discovered a lump in my breast. When I was diagnosed with breast cancer, tears fell uncontrollably. To console myself, I sat and sewed a wee bear with a "mastectomy." She is so soft and made of recycled beaver.

With the help of my supportive family, I elected to have surgery and treatment in my native New Zealand. *Saffron* was my constant companion and was under my arm as I went into surgery. Because of the early detection and two successful procedures, the removal of the lump and chemotherapy, the doctors had saved my breast. My healing therapy came from the one thing I loved to do most — making Teddy Bears.

BEAR MAKING HINTS:
1. Transfer the pattern on to the backside of course sandpaper (60 Grit), twice each piece, reversing one. Then cut out, using "old" scissors. Hot glue the backsides together. The sandpaper sticks to the fabric piece and now it is easy to mark around. It needs no pins or weights to keep in place and is strong for repeated use.
2. To store pattern pieces together, make a hole at the top and hang pieces for each bear on closable wire shower curtain hooks. To avoid mix-up of pattern pieces, one curtain hook contains all the pieces for one bear.

70. Denzil Laurence has achieved international recognition with her personalized themed Teddy Bears. Pictured with Denzil are two of her most popular characters, *Phantom of the Opera* (left), *Sherlock Holmes* (right). To ensure accuracy with the designs and style of clothing Denzil researches each character in her local library. *Photograph by Peggy Baughman.*

71. *Bishop Bear.* 1995. 15in (38cm); golden tan mohair; Plexiglas eyes; fully jointed; self standing. Cape and robe are red velvet lined in gold lamé. The staff, jewelry, and cross are handmade by the artist. One-of-a-kind. Custom order for Bishop Juan Baladad.

Tammie Lawrence
TAMMIE'S TEDDYS

72. Tammie Lawrence has been delighting collectors with her authentic antique reproduction bears since 1981. *Photograph by Paul Beave.*

73. (Left) *Alphonse.* 1994. 16in (41cm); extremely tattered and worn cinnamon colored mohair; antique shoe button eyes; fully jointed. Wearing a worn black wool coat, antique shoes and glasses. (Right) *Elouise.* 1995. 16in (41cm); extremely tattered and worn pale gold mohair; antique shoe button eyes; fully jointed. Dressed in an antique pale blue dress, tattered straw hat trimmed in old flowers, and antique shoes. *Alphonse* and *Elouise* are limited editions of 25 each. *Photograph by George Comito.*

I began making bears in early 1981. I experimented with a store bought pattern just to see how a bear went together. I was very frustrated with trying to work with someone else's pattern. (This wasn't unusual, since I have always had difficulty taking directions on how to do a specific thing and always preferred to do it my way!

After seeing an antique bear in Bialosky's Identification book that I loved, I tried to make my own pattern. It was a disaster — looking nothing at all like the picture, but it started me on the road of developing my own original patterns and the look I wanted.

All my bears are antique reproductions, prior to the 1930s. I use nothing but natural fibers such as mohair and wools to make the bears. Then I dress them in antique clothing and trims. Many are one-of-a-kind, as I become very bored with edition bears when I have to make the same piece over and over. I have a really difficult time making the same two bears look exactly alike. I don't even like to try. I will use the same pattern and the same fabric, but they are never the same.

I do all the work myself from designing the patterns to writing out the shipping labels. I prefer to do it this way so I have full and complete control over all aspects of my business. If it gets to be too much, I just refuse to take on anymore. I am often told by other artists that I am making a mistake by not allowing my business to grow to the size it could, if I had a staff helping me. I know I could earn more money if I did, but that is not my main goal. I want to continue to love what I do, have fun doing it, keep the bills paid, have a little extra to play with, and sleep well at night. I really love the fact that I seem to be doing something that brings a lot of happiness to people around me.

I make no more than 25 bears a month, with the exception of the Christmas season. My goal is never to overload the market with my bears, but, at the same time, never have a long waiting list for the customers to endure. I don't believe in making customers wait for months for one of my bears.

Prices for my bears start around $60 for a 4in (10cm) undressed tattered mohair bear and go up to nearly $1000 for the 40in (101cm) distressed mohair bear, fully dressed in antique clothing and trims.

I must admit that one of my hardest tasks in bear making has been dealing with the unfortunate, dishonest people who find it necessary to infringe on my original ideas. It really hurts me when I hear or see another, so called artist, boldly steal from an original design that I have spent endless hours developing. However, over the years I have found that those dishonest people never endure the hardships of this business and they fade away pretty quickly. It is only the ones who really love what they do and go about it in a sincere and honest way that endure it all and continue forward.

I have a small list of stores I sell to, worldwide, that total no more than 20 altogether. Recently I began offering all bears through retail mail order. I do not attend shows myself, but some of the stores that carry my bears do.

I want to keep right on doing what I have been doing since 1981. If it ever stops being enjoyable, I have no doubt that I will quit and go on to something new.

40

Tammie Lawrence
TAMMIE'S TEDDYS

74. (Left to right) *Gardening Genevieve Rabbit, Earnestina Eggbasket* and *Primrose Panda.* 1994-1995. 9in (23cm). These unique characters are crafted in distressed mohair, with long narrow fully jointed bodies and shoe button eyes. Each animal is trimmed in new and old trims according to what suits their personalities. Produced in various sized editions. *Photograph by George Comito.*

Rose Leshko
BEAR VALLEY BEARS

I began making bears for fun in 1987 when a dear friend was teaching how to make Teddy Bears. The following year it turned into a business.

My bears are from 6—30in (15—76cm). They are always fully-jointed, made of mohair, stuffed, or pellet filled. I am best known for my bears' faces and expressions.

My husband helps me cut, stuff, and joint my bears. I do the rest of the work and produce 250-275 bears a year. Usually, I do about eight to 10 shows a year where I sometimes teach workshops for those in attendance.

My biggest pleasure is seeing customer's reaction to bears. I also find great rewards in donating my bears to charities and knowing that I've helped someone financially or cheered them up.

BEAR MAKING HINTS: When using patterns to make Teddy Bear clothing, use baby doll clothing patterns. They fit Teddy Bears really well!

75. Rose Leshko enjoys enhancing her bears character by concocting fun outfits for them.

76. (Left) *Heather.* 1995. 18in (46cm); gold distressed mohair; black glass eyes; fully jointed. (Right) *Winston.* 1995. 24in (61cm); white string mohair; black glass eyes; fully jointed. One-of-a-kind.

Rita Loeb
RITA LOEB'S TINY TEDDY COMPANY

I've always been a bear collector and began taking classes at bear conventions in 1988 and 1989. When I took a class from the renowned miniature Teddy Bear artist Sandy Williams in 1990, that was the real start.

My specialties are miniature bears with fat tummies. Some are undressed to show off their figures. The dressed ones have their costumes incorporated into their body designs. Each bear has an ultrasuede tag attached at mid-back. Some of these fat little guys have a sad pout.

I sell only direct retail. I am the Tiny Teddy Company and do all the work personally, making about 100 bears a year. Most of the bears do not have limited quantities. Their prices range from $70 to $135 apiece.

BEAR MAKING HINTS: Persistence and desire is 90% of getting the job done. Try to go on and finish without looking too closely at the little mistakes along the way.

77. Rita Loeb works at home with the help of her five Shih-Tzu dogs and two of her cats. When exhibiting at a show, Rita takes about twenty little bears. Her entire inventory fits neatly in a container about the size of a one pound candy box.

78. *P.J. Jammy Bears.* 1993. (Left, and center 2-1/2in (6cm); (right) 2in (5cm); various colors of upholstery fabric; round glass bead eyes; fully jointed. Jammies are an integral part of the body. Each bear comes with its own tinier "Ted." *Photograph by Stacey Stucky.*

Tracy Main
TEDDYS BY TRACY

79. In addition to creating adorable little bears, Tracy Main is very involved in the supply end of the Teddy Bear business.

I met Durae Allen at a doll and bear show, saw her work, and thought it would be fun to make bears myself. So, for the past four years, I have been making about 75 to 100 plain and dressed miniature bears a year, selling them both retail and wholesale. I do at least five shows a year. My bears range from 3/4—4in (2—10cm) and sell for between $30.00 and $100.00 each.

I am very involved in the supply end of the business. In 1991, when I started making miniature Teddy Bears, it was nearly impossible to find the right fabric. When I saw the upholstery velvet that a few artists were using, I discovered that there wasn't one person or central place that sold a lot of it. I was determined to find some of this good material. When I finally found some, little did I know how many others wanted it too. So now, I have about 50 different colors and styles and am even trying to have a longer pile manufactured. (We also carry other tools, silk ribbons, eyes, joints, pocket watch cases, kits, and ultrasuedes).

I myself teach workshops at local shops and shows, and highly recommend you taking a class or workshop if you are new to bear making.

80. Bears. 1995. 2-1/2in (6cm); upholstery velvet bodies; black onyx eyes; fully jointed. A representation of Tracy Main's precious little teddy designs.

43

81. Diane Martin's love of the Victorian era and the style of clothes during that period is portrayed in the outfits she designs for her bears.

Diane L. Martin
BLUE MOON BEARS

I made my first bear for my daughter in 1987. It was out of my pink and white childhood quilt. In the beginning my bears were made of old quilts and coats, but for the last six years, I've worked exclusively with imported mohair.

In April of 1988, I found an antique baby slip in a store near my home. I put it on a bear at my first show in Nevada City that same week. I had such an overwhelming response to that bear, that I've been hunting for and using vintage doll and baby clothes on my bears ever since. They seem to bring out the best in each other.

I work on bears entirely by myself, except for the occasional help from my children, Christopher, age 9 and Emily, age 7. They make 10¢ a bear for removing the pins from the bears after their first sewing.

All Blue Moon Bears have a mother-of-pearl button in their left ear. Each button is hand-painted with a Blue Moon and the year it was created. I also sew a hand-signed ultra-suede tag into the back of one leg or on smaller bears, the back of the body.

My bears, by the nature of their costuming and accessorizing, are all individual. I have made limited editions in the past and plan to again, but they have been and will be limited to an edition of 13 because that is my lucky number. Plus, I don't like to do the same bear over and over.

I exhibit at six to eight shows a year and make an average of 200 bears a year (sometimes a few more, mostly a lot less!). They range in price from $95 for a 10in (25cm) in a lace collar to $650 for a 40in (102cm) bear in a complete vintage dress.

Sometimes I barter with my bears. I don't usually trade my bears for others, but for quilts, antiques, other artist's creations, and especially for vintage clothes, shoes, and accessories.

It's hard to part with my bears sometimes. My favorite break during my workday is the walk to my mailbox and the hope that I'll get a letter and picture from another collector. I have an old leather photo album that I keep most of these photos in and it's fun to look back, especially to the oldest ones.

My hope and dream is that 100 years from now, one of my great grandchildren will see a Blue Moon Bear and smile because they'll know their great-grandma made that bear a century ago!

82. *Sophie* (sitting) and *Emily* (standing). 1995. 13in (33cm); mohair bodies; glass eyes; fully jointed. One-of-a-kind.

44

Randy Martin Sr.
LIL' BROTHER'S BEARS

I used to make fishing lures and frame antique movie ads but now my forte is miniature bears, as well as other unique creatures.

My bears and other critters consist of vintage upholstery fabric, black onyx or glass bead eyes, durable plastic disc joints, ultra suede pads, all new cotton batting for stuffing, and painstakingly developed charming faces!

My bears, which I mainly sell through the mail and wholesale to just two shops, currently retail from $100 to $225. Most of them are 2-1/2in (6cm), however some of them are actually as small as 1-1/2in (4cm).

One of my more unique creatures is *Humboldt Penguin.* I began making *Humboldt Penguins* when I became involved with helping my good friend and fellow artist, Millie Gage raise needed funds to save that particular species of penguin. My first finished penguin was a donation prototype which was raffled to raise funds for the endangered "Humboldt." This began a limited edition of ten.

I still produce a variety of other penguin species, however, no more Humboldt's will ever be offered for sale. I mostly produce one-of-a-kind miniatures. However, I sometimes offer limited editions as well as open editions. The limited editions usually do not exceed 25.

My wife, Cristan, does a wonderful job of assisting me with shows, of which we go to three or five a year. Since I began making bears in 1993, I have made 60 to 150 annually.

The reason I call my bears "Lil' Brother's Bears" is because I was inspired and encouraged by my big sister, Debbie Kesling.

BEAR MAKING HINTS: If you are a new bear artist, it is a good idea to accept constructive criticism; but don't let the tastes and opinions of others dictate how your bear should look. We each have unique qualities and the rewards are great when an artist decides to "get off the beaten path and take chances."

83. In addition to his tiny teddies Randy Martin Sr. also creates a menagerie of other creatures. This photograph depicts the intense concentration and attention to detail Randy affords his bears. *Photograph by Roger Marlin.*

84. (Left) *King Penguin* (Baby) 1995. 1-1/2in (4cm); body hand dyed brown upholstery fabric; Fimo® beak and feet; ultrasuede paw pads; antique cut-glass bead eyes; fully jointed. (Center) *Giant (Tiny) Panda.* 1995. 2in (5cm); body hand-dyed black and white upholstery fabric; hand tinting around the eyes; ultrasuede paw pads; antique cut-glass beads eyes; fully jointed. (Right) *King Penguin* (Adult). 1995. 1-7/8in (5cm); hand tinted upholstery fabric; Fimo® beak (beak is hand painted) and feet, antique cut-glass bead eyes; jointed arms and head. *King Penguins* (Adult and Baby) are a very accurate representation of real penguins. They are also self standing which make them easily displayed. Sold in sets (Adult and Baby). Limited edition of 25 sets.

45

90. This portrait of Helen and Roger Morris surrounded by some of the creations, illustrates how their shared love of art and animals contribute to the unique and beautiful work they create together.

We were on vacation in Kansas during Thanksgiving of 1987. A very special friend, Virginia Quinn, told us about "Good Bears of the World." She showed us her collection and publications. Before we knew it we were visiting every Teddy Bear store we could find. After falling in love with artist bears, Roger was the one who started checking out all the information on Teddy Bears and their construction.

We both design our own bears and other critters. Once in a while we combine efforts in what we call "Ars" or "You & Me" bears. These are usually done for the three doll and Teddy Bear shows we attend in Puyallup, Washington.

Every December we create 10—12 new items for the upcoming year to be sold wholesale. All our exclusively hand-sewn designs are our very own creations, mainly 4in (10cm) and under. In 1994 we produced and sold just over 400 critters.

You can find our bears in six other countries and more than 200 shops. Fabrics used are nylon, rayon, mohair, and vintage goods. Hand embroidered details complete the character of each design.

BEAR MAKING HINTS:
1. Since fabrics vary in construction, adjust your stitching both in length and depth for both strength and best look.
2. Some fabrics need coating; some on the edge only; others completely with a white craft glue; and some need another complete coating after sewing, but before turning.

91. *The Circus.* 1995. This magnificent array of animals portrays just a small selection of the tremendous variety that is produced by this talented couple.

Cecilia Moudree
ZOOLATANA BEAR CO.

After Christmas 1980, when Santa didn't bring me the Steiff *Papa Bear* I wanted, I sat down with one of my old bears and a piece of Saran Wrap and a marking pen and traced a pattern. I made this first bear from dark purple plush and gave it to a friend who admired it. Her encouraging words inspired me to make more.

And have I made more! Approximately 500 a year and they are all fully articulated mohair bears, 2—36in (5—91cm). They range in price from $100 to $700 and each has a Zoolatana Bear Co. cloth tag sewn into the back seam. They also have hang tags of ultrasuede with the number, date, logo, and product information. I sign bears only at personal appearances.

My son is responsible for the name of my company. We used to live in Missoula, Montana when he was little. Because that was a mouthful for a 2-1/2 year old, he would say we lived in "Zoola-tana." That's how the name was born.

92. Cecilia Moudree refrains from trying to anticipate what collectors will want to buy, and tries to stick to her desire to create the kind of bears she loves. This has proven to be a good decision as her bears are highly sought after by collectors around the world and have won many awards.

Pat Murphy
MURPHY BEARS

I began making bears part time in 1984. By 1990 it became a full time business. I make and design all the bears myself, but since 1993 my daughter has been helping with some cutting and sewing. Each year, I produce between 300 to 400 traditional style bears with antique accessories and attend 10 to 12 shows a year. There is an open line made annually, as well as several limited editions and 50 to 75 one-of-a-kinds that are only sold at shows.

Most of my bears are mohair and a few are vintage alpaca and rayon. Parts of my bears I stuff with excelsior. It gives the feet and paws great definition and helps to sculpt wonderful heads and muzzles.

They range in size from 12—28in (31—71cm) and are priced from $150 to $550. Murphy Bears are tagged on the hump of the back.

I am pleased to have achieved respect and friendship of many other talented bear artists and equally pleased to boast a very broad base of clientele in the USA and overseas. My satisfaction comes from the development of a personal creative style. I think of the heads as sculpture and mold them into that final shape and "look."

BEAR MAKING HINTS:
1. Stuff bears' heads, paws, and feet \ with excelsior to give them a great shape.
2. Fray-check is a must for each bear's muzzle as it gives added strength and rigidity to the bear's nose. This way, if you have to take out a nose, it's easier on a firm muzzle.

Top to Bottom: **93.** Pat Murphy feels making bears should come from the heart and soul and the personal desire to express oneself.
94. (Left) *Keanu.* 1994. 15in (38cm); hand dyed light beige distressed mohair; antiqued glass eyes; fully jointed; excelsior stuffed; squeaker encased in body. (Right) *Rusty.* 1994. 20in (51cm); ultra-sparse cinnamon colored distressed mohair; antiqued glass eyes; fully jointed; excelsior stuffed; growler encased in body; antiqued leather paw pads.

93

94

49

95. Kathy Myers and her daughter Kellisa share in their love of Teddy Bears. Kellisa's favorite bears however, are of course the ones lovingly made by her Mom. The bear in Kellisa's arms was made by her Mom and named Kellisa in honor of her wonderful daughter. Although Kathy is well-known for her beautiful teddies made of recycled vintage furs, pictured on the left are two of her larger bears she makes from mohair.

96. (Top-clockwise) *Little LilliAnn, Mandy Panda, Simone, Cubby.* 1993-1995. Bears range in size from 3—10in (8—25cm); recycled vintage mink bodies; glass or antique shoebutton eyes; fully jointed.

I prefer to discuss each teddy personally beforehand because I think of each of my Teddy Bears as soft sculpture...a huggable work of art.

I specialize in recycled vintage fur Teddy Bears. This is an odd profession for a person who has been a vegetarian for more than 20 years. But, then again, maybe it gives me a greater sensitivity and more inspiration to create my furry "children." My bears are all recycled from vintage fur coats, stoles, and collars. I believe that the "spirit" of the animal somehow lives on. It feels wonderful to release that spirit from its "coat-bondage" and transform it back into a creature that is once again respected and loved. All Teddy Bears are alive in their own magical way, but my real fur teddies seem to possess a special life within them. Because they were once living, breathing creatures I do not feel like I create them as much as I allow them to be reborn.

Like many other Teddy Bear artists who are also mothers, I was first inspired to make a bear because I loved my daughter so much that I wanted to create something very special just for her. The odd thing was that after I completed my first bear, making bears became an obsession for me. I just could not stop thinking about my next design. And the next. And the next.

Collectors seem to love my bears because of the wonderful sweet faces that I manage to find hidden under all that fur. I scissor-sculpt my bear's faces and I also truly fall in love with each one of their sweet little faces. Sometimes it's hard to give them up for adoption, but I know that they are going to loving homes.

Due to supply and demand, I prefer to sell my bears retail only. Although, there are a few persistent Teddy Bear shops which occasionally will have one or two of my bears available for adoption.

I spend 8—12 hours on each bear because most, if not all, of each bear is stitched by hand. This is usually necessary because of the small size. I have spent as much as five hours just taking apart an old coat and preparing it. All of my bears are lined to give them extra strength. I use glass eyes and I stitch the noses. My annual production is about 250 bears a year. Each is tagged behind their left ear. When I turned professional, I started numbering my bears consecutively. Usually I charge from $65 to $125 for my services.

Making bears not only allows me to express myself creatively, but it gives me much needed rejuvenation throughout my day. At the age of six, my daughter, Kellisa, was diagnosed with Cystic Fibrosis. Caring for a chronically ill child can be so overwhelming that being a Teddy Bear artist has been a true blessing for so many reasons...most of all it allows me time to care for my child myself.

BEAR MAKING HINTS: If you are troubled by tendinitis in your hands, do not work too many long hours. Prepare your hands with a moist heat compress to loosen up your muscles. Wear "handeze" gloves and warm them up before putting them on. Take a lot of breaks to rest your hands and if you do feel pain at the end of the day, apply ice to bring down the swelling. When you are not working, exercise your fingers and hands.

Sue Newlin
SUE NEWLIN ORIGINALS

In 1981, I learned to make jointed bears from Linda Speigel-Lohre of Bearly There. She took my first 9in (23cm) Bear Couple with overalls (*John Travis and Nicole*), along with my *Bear on Wheels* to one of her store accounts and came back with an order!

My whole family is artistic. They all draw, paint, and create continually. Besides bears, I have done stained glass, drawing, and am currently working on a line of ceramics.

My mohair bears 7in (18cm)retail at $75. The prices incrementally increase (15in/38cm, $175) (22in/56cm, $250). I produce about 110 bears a year and make whatever I'm in the mood to do. I try to leave myself open to repeat bears. The last eight years, I've done all the work myself This year I have cut way back and am going to do only one or two shows a year. This way I can concentrate on creating things I like more than concentrating on volume. I hope to spend more of my time working on my ceramics.

BEAR MAKING HINTS: Save the lids of greeting card boxes for the clear plastic and use it for patterns. It's easy to cut and write on and its durable. You can also buy it at some stationery stores or printers.

98. (Left) *Henry.* 1995. 22in (56cm); tipped dark brown mohair; glass eyes; fully jointed. (Center) *Sawyer.* 1992. 18in (46cm); pale beige mohair; glass eyes; fully jointed. (Right) *Scotty.* 1991. 15in (38cm); rust colored mohair; suede paw pads; glass eyes; fully jointed. (Bottom) *Old Sonny.* 1994. 8-1/2in (22cm); pale cream colored mohair; suede paw pads; glass eyes; fully jointed; mohair is distressed and shaved for worn, loved appearance; embroidered "patches" applied to mohair.

97. Sue Newlin looks with affection and approval at her newly created white *Scotty* bear.

51

99

100

Beverly Matteson Port
BEVERLY PORT ORIGINALS

I probably liked Teddy Bears before I was born. I had a big brown and gold bear who was my friend. We had many visits and tea parties; but when we moved a big packing box was lost; it contained my special Teddy Bear and my mom's best china and silver — never to be found! Thus began the "Teddy Bear Trauma" for me. I thought no other could take his place and wished that he would miraculously appear. Perhaps the best part of making Teddy Bears is recapturing some of that happiness from childhood in every bear I create.

Cloth was the first medium I used for small hand-sewn Teddy Bears. I first made small one-piece felt bears; then jointed velour and velvet ones. I also modeled teddies for ornaments and figurines. I have progressed through the years, making larger sizes, using both acrylics and mohair materials. I have combined fabric faces with sculptured modeled mouths with tongues. Some even have teeth. Glass eyes are now inset into the eye sockets. I've made mechanical bears with heads that turn by moving their tail; others with tails that wind a music box and other novelty bears including candy containers, perfume bears, bears-on-wheels, patchwork bears, characters bears and multi-movement automatons with music. Over the years they have become more detailed.

I work with porcelain, wax and cloth in both doll making and bear making.

I actually coined the term "Teddy Bear Artist" and have seen the field expand greatly in the last 15 years. I am honored to be called the "First Lady of Teddy Bear Artists" and "mother of the Bear Artist Movement" by leading authors and my peers in the field.

Since early on, I have written articles and made personal appearances. I gave the first slide program to a large UFDC (United Federation of Doll Clubs) in 1972. The largest group I ever gave a slide program to was at the Palmer House in Chicago, where 1800 people registered in 1986. I even gave "Teddy Bear Health Hazard" workshops during the 1980s at various conventions and shows.

Not only have I been chosen the winner of numerous awards, I am now a judge for both the Golden Teddy's as well as the TOBY® Awards. I'm also a DOTY® award judge and have judged Teddy Bear exhibits at conventions from coasts to coast, England, and Canada.

Continued on page 53.

Top to Bottom: **99.** Beverly Matteson Port, truly the pioneer in the artist bear world, has been generously sharing her talents and her time since she began creating bears in the late 1960s. Beverly poses with *Miss Emily Bearkin*, The Epicurean Teddy. *Photograph by John Paul Port.*
100. (Back) *Tedwina Cinnabär.* 1974-1995. 14in (35cm); rust tipped plush; sculpted and carved porcelain face (fired in Kiln); china-painted features (fired in many layers to obtain depth and color); glass eyes; fully jointed. (Left) *Baby Brat.* 1975-1995. 4in (10cm); vintage short golden plush; glass eyes. *Muzzle* (including nose) is sculptured of hard composition with open mouth, teeth and tongue. Then fabric of head is glued around nose and mouth. (Center) *Tiny Tedwina.* 1974-1995. 3in (8cm); vintage velvety velour; sculpted porcelain face; painted "googlie" eyes; jointed arms and legs. *Tedwina* has a tail that activates a mechanism that turns her head back and forth. *Photograph by John Paul Port.*

52

I am the only person who works for me. I am president, vice-president, product development chairperson, distributor, and "chief cook and bottle washer."

Perhaps my hardest task is keeping my studio in good condition, to find everything readily when I need it. My work areas are generally messy. I have a profusion of supplies and sewing machines, including an 1890s Singer treadle that sews beautifully, up to a 1990s electronic "miracle machine," Each works best with certain fabrics.

The handmade Teddy Bear has two categories: 1) Those by Teddy Bear makers who use a commercial pattern or patterns sold by another individual specially for reproduction by others. In this case, the bear should have the source of its pattern on its label and 2) those by Teddy Bear artists who use only their own originally designed patterns and can have their work copyrighted in the Library of Congress.

When I create a bear, I'm trying for a look of timelessness, something artistic in expression, but capable of evoking an emotional response. Bears are like little people — "animal people" — and each one has a distinct and different personality. Happy, sulky, sad or any other emotion can be evinced by a subtle shaping of the head, turn of the mouth, set to the eye — an intangible "something" that sets them apart, one from another, much as human people.

BEAR MAKING HINTS:

1. Beginning bear makers can find patterns in commercial pattern books by McCalls, Simplicity, Vogue, Butterick, etc. Look for kits and patterns in stores, clubs, and magazines. Many books are out with a variety of patterns and projects. Hobby House Press, Inc. has a Teddy Bear catalog listing many books and patterns.

2. Never take a pattern from someone else's bear, without specific permission.

3. To begin designing your own pattern, begin with a flat two-piece or unjointed bear and then progress to a jointed one. Begin with a small bear, as it isn't easy to make adjustments on huge ones at the start.

4. Protect your original designs and mark your bears with a copyright symbol, your name and date. Register in the Library of Congress.

5. Cut plush and upholstery fabric carefully; vacuum frequently or cut it outside, as the tiny particles tend to float in the air.

6. Get a good polyester fiberfill with long fibers and a smooth, springy feel to it. Pull apart your bear "filling" and see if it too releases debris into the air.

101

102

Top to Bottom: **101.** *The Cosmic Puppeteer with Ima and Youra Baerhart.* 1990. 20in (50cm) overall height. This magnificent one-of-a-kind musical and mechanical piece was created by Beverly as her charity donation for "The Teddy Bear Homecoming in the Heartland" held in Clarion in 1990. Key wound mechanism activates music and the movement. *Photograph by Beverly Matteson Port.*
102. A representation of the super eminent and creative workmanship of the gifted and accomplished teddy bear artists — The Port Family. (Back left) *Theodore B Bear.* 1974-1995. 15in (38cm). (Back right) *Sarafina Sunflower Bearkin.* 1978-1995. 14in (36cm). (Right) *Olde.* 1960. 8in (20cm). (Left front) John Paul Port. *Lucky Rainbow.* 1994. 12in (31cm). (Right front) Kimberlee Port. *Shimmer E. Rainbow.* 1991. 3in (8cm). *Photograph by Norman Garner.*

53

Olwyn and William Price
WIL-O-WYN BEARS

109. The gentle and sweet personalities of Olwyn and William Price can be seen in the faces of their "Wil-O-Wyn" Bear creations. Each endearing face of their bears is hand-sculptured in clay and hand-painted.

Our first bear was born in January of 1989. I kept two of the first seven and gave away five. We sold our first bear March 1, 1989 for $75. The way we got started was first being aware of the use of Teddy Bears as decorating accessories in magazines. Around that time we met Steve Schutt (Clarion, Iowa) at a bear and doll shop. He was demonstrating bear making and that gave us the incentive to try ourselves.

We don't make many bears a year, about 20 all told and we average two or three shows a year. What we make are one-of-a-kind collectibles with individual sculptured clay baked faces. Most are mohair and a few are German acrylic fur. We copyright each of our bears which sell for $150 to $400 and range in size from 6—24in (15—61cm) tall.

As a child, I had a host of dolls but never a Teddy Bear. Now I am retired and in my second childhood. Every room in our house is filled with these happy creatures. They are not necessarily all of our own making. We also collect other artist bears.

BEAR MAKING HINTS:
1. Sew in all paw pads by hand to assure a smooth wrinkle free appearance.
2. Use a small fishing tackle box to keep bolts, cotter pins, washers, tools, and other pertinent items.

110. *Tedman Lovewell.* 1994. 18in (46cm); medium blonde mohair; glass eyes; fully jointed; hand sculptured hand-painted (acrylic) clay face. Clothing, cushion, and artwork by Olwyn. Easel, stool, pail, chair, mirror, helmet and base made by William Price. One-of-a-kind.

56

Michelle Province-Gesher
ITTY BITTY SMALL
ORIGINALS & PATTERN CO.

I began making bears as a hobby in 1988 when I was 17 years old. It wasn't until 1991 that I began producing bears for resale. The first bear I bought, which inspired me to make my own, was made by Rita Loeb of Tiny Teddy Company.

I've been drawing and sculpting since I was big enough to hold a pencil and work with clay. I've worked as an illustrator and logo designer. I received my diploma in Graphic Design in 1992. My current occupation of Registered Dental Assistant may seem distant from my avocation, but the job actually requires an ability for sculpting and molding.

I primarily design miniature bears, but have recently expanded my creativity to include mini-rabbits, monkeys, elephants, and other "bear friends."

Although I do the designing and prototypes of my creations, there's much more to the business than

111. Michelle Province-Gesher's primary focus is on patterns and kits, but all of her designs are available in finished form.

I can handle. After I finish a new design and have a workable product, I draw exact illustrations and pattern templates. My father (Mike Province) scans the artwork into his computer, my mother (Lacy Province) uses the computer to combine artwork with detailed instructions into booklet form. My mother also takes care of all business matters. My husband (Russell Gesher) helps with retail sales at shows, ideas, and support. Phil McMahan, a family friend and photo editor at the *San Diego Union-Tribune* does our photography. The finished product is a clean, neat, and professional booklet that goes to the printer. It's extremely important to approach this as a professional business venture.

I only have time to produce about 100 custom bears each year, since my business has become more pattern oriented in the last couple of years. I try to create at least one new pattern a month. My primary focus is patterns and kits, but all of my designs are available in finished form with a 4—5 week lead time after taking an order. Finished bears retail for $60 to $125 and range from 2—5in (5— 13cm). They are made of various materials, including mohair, upholstery fabric, and ultra-suede. Kits range from $10 to $20 and patterns are all $6.

One of my goals is to open my own shop, teach classes, and offer another avenue of sales to other Teddy Bear Artists.

BEAR MAKING HINTS:
1. When sewing bear parts by machine, sew around each piece twice. This will ensure that extra bit of strength in the seams.
2. Take your time. Don't be discouraged. Each bear will be different with its own style and personality.

112. (Left) *Bumble Bear.* 1994. 3-1/2in (9cm); upholstery fabric body; ultra suede vest; glass bead eyes; fully jointed. (Center front) *Piggin's.* 1995. 2-1/2in (6cm); upholstery fabric body; ultra suede scarf; glass bead eyes; stationary arms and legs; swivel head. (Center back) *Tug.* 1995. 4-3/8in (11cm); upholstery fabric body, hand-painted strips; ultra suede nose; glass bead eyes; fully jointed; flexible tail. (Right) *Emmett.* 1995. 1-7/8in (5cm); upholstery fabric body; ultra suede mane and tip of tail (removable button tail); glass bead eyes; unjointed. *Photograph by Phil McMahan.*

I made my first bear about 25 years ago, but it wasn't until six years ago, while living in Las Cruces, New Mexico, that I sold my first bear. I had begun making my bears just for my children, then 15 years later I began collecting bears. I was encouraged by my friend (and wonderful artist of adorable dogs and other animals) to start making bears to sell to support my habit.

I make fully-jointed mohair bears with glass eyes, which are mostly one-of-a-kind or very limited editions. I specialize in antique and handmade props such as old boxes and quilts, which is appropriate since I also make doll houses and quilts. In fact, I own a quilt business, but after ten years, I had to put it on hold as I don't have time.

I've written for *Teddy Bear Review*, taught classes, was nominated for Golden Teddy in 1992, won National Teddy Roosevelt Bear Contest in 1993, won TOBY® in 1993, and was invited to participate in the 1993 Disneyland Doll and Bear Show. I must admit I want to be famous in my field. This means being on the cover of the magazine, winning more contests, and doing more elaborate studio pieces.

Even though I am the only worker, I do collaborate with a couple other artists on complicated pieces. I usually make the bear and they make the pet or miniature bear to go with it. They are then sold as a set.

I make about 200 bears a year and exhibit at about eight shows per year, mostly in the Maryland and Virginia area. I charge from \$125—\$1000 for my bears. I use sewn in hangtags to identify my bears. In addition, each bear has a sterling silver paw charm in the left ear.

BEAR MAKING HINTS: Teddy's soul lives in his head. Cut out, stuff, and finish off the bear's head first. Then, if he doesn't have the right look, you haven't wasted much fur.

113. Susan Redstreake Geary was proud to be one of the invited Teddy Bear artists to exhibit her work at Disneyland's Teddy Bear and Doll Classic in 1993. Her cute baby bear *Carly*, which she holds here, was created in a limited edition of 25 especially for the event.

114. Susan Redstreake Geary and Bonnie Moose (Bears, Hares, and Other Wares), combined their talents by working on this enchanting piece together. *"Love is More Precious When Given Away."* 1995. Bear. 27in (69cm). Bear wears a dress and hat (fabric pictures puppies), white antique pinafore, baby shoes. A music box encased in body plays "All I Ask of You." Bear holds a basket of mohair jointed puppies (two with open mouths). One puppy is hiding in her purse. Not only does she shed a tear, she also has a sterling silver paw charm in her ear. Limited edition of three.

Monty and Joe Sours
THE BEAR LADY

We have always been interested in restoring and creating antiques, ranging from furniture to complete houses. Joe is nationally noted for his recreations of antique firearms from the flintlock period. So, when our friend, Jackie Taylor, gave us our first bear as a gift and then showed us how to make one of our own, we were hooked. We spent a year studying the features of both old and new Teddy Bears and even spent a great deal of time studying live bears. We made our first bear in 1980.

We try to combine the features of the live bears while retaining the warm cuddliness of the Teddy Bear. We have developed a unique system using cast pewter weights to produce a true free standing bear. The two of us do all the work on our bears (400—500 a year) with no outside help. Any one who could meet our quality and design standards should be our competition, not our employee. The two of us have a synergistic relationship that produces a better bear than either could create alone.

We maintain a line of 14—18 open edition designs that are produced in a wide range of fabrics. Sometimes we do limited editions for our retailers. Most of our bears sell for $125 (7-1/2in {19cm}) to $350 (18in {46cm}). We also produce bears from woven mohair plush that range from $2500 —$3500.

Over the years we have won a number of awards at shows, most notably the Golden Teddy Award in 1992. One of our handwoven bears *Horace Eugene* was featured on the cover of *Teddy Bear and Friends®* (February 1995). You can find our bears in several U.S. museums as well as the Teddy Bear Museum in Stratford-Upon-Avon in England and the new Teddy Bear museum Yoshihiro Sekiguchi opened in Japan.

Perhaps the greatest pleasure we have received from bear making was the success in creating a mohair plush bear totally from scratch. We spun the yarn and wove the plush fabric as well as the flat weave fabric for the paws and the yarn for the nose and mouth. The fabric was hand dyed naturally with walnut hulls and oak bark.

Continued on page 60.

115. Monty and Joe Sours successfully developed the unique task in creating mohair plush totally from scratch. Monty (left) is holding *Jackie,* one of the artist's hand woven plush bears. Joe (right) holds *Horace Eugene,* another of their hand-woven creations. Left of the foreground is Casper, the Llama, who will provide the fiber for this creative couple's next weaving project — an alpaca bear.

116. The most timely and critical process in creating mohair plush for making bears is the spinning of the yarn. Over 1-1/4 miles of yarn, the finest of kite string is needed for a 14in (36cm) bear. Monty Sours emphasizes that the final fabric is only as good as the yarn used to make it with.

59

117. After the hair is spun into yarn it is then threaded onto the loom. In an exact order to weave a piece of fabric 20in (51cm) wide, 1,020 strands of yarn must be placed in the lettles of the loom. This is done in two segments as two weaving processes take place at the same time to weave plush fabric.

BEAR MAKING HINTS:
1. Keep one of your first bears. It will keep you humble as you progress and can be used after you have perfected your product to show new artists that you too started at the bottom.
2. This is our step-by-step method in making mohair from scratch:
A. Shear an angora goat.
B. After washing hair, tease it to separate fibers.
C. Place on wire rack to dry.
D. Card the dry fibers.
E. Spin the yarn. It takes 880 pieces of yarn per warp for a piece of fabric 20 inches (51cm) wide.
F. Weave the backing at the same time the plush is woven into it.
G. Use wooden spacers to control the length of the plush.
H. Cut the loops so the twist can be removed and plush changed back to hair.
I. Wash the fabric in soap and water.
J. Dye fabric in natural solution.
K. Card fabric to orient the nap.
L. Place on smooth surface; tease for texture and dry.

118. (Left) *Albert.* 1993. 18in (46cm); gold mohair; glass eyes; fully jointed. Wearing a bright red tie made by the artists. (Center) *Waldo.* 1993. 14in (36cm); medium brown mohair; glass eyes; fully jointed. (Right) *Christopher.* 10in (25cm); honey colored mohair; glass eyes; fully jointed. Each bear is designed to be free standing.

M. Michele Thorp
MOSSY LOG STUDIO

I received my first bear, Andy, for Christmas in 1945. He has been my major inspiration in my bear making efforts!

Over the past fifty years I have been doing art work in one form or another. I have a M.S. in Education with a major in Art Education from the University of Oregon. I taught arts and crafts classes in the public schools, for local art businesses, and in my own studio. Part of that artistic expression was in making bears for my four children.

I am best known for my character bears, bears on all fours, a Teddy Bear purse, muff, and rugs. I do grizzlies, black bears, polar bears, and pandas. I use the same source material for designing bears as that used in painting wildlife scenes and photos of real bears.

Lately I am almost as involved in paper doll design as I am in bear making. Most of my paper dolls are of my own bears in the Mossy Log Woods story line. I also do notecards and stationery depicting my bears. I am having some success marketing photo prints of paintings of my bears, dolls, and other toys. My latest adventure is in T-shirt design.

119. Michele Thorp feels an artist's best work comes from the inner depths of the individual artist.

Teddy Bear and Friends® and *Teddy Bear Review* have both published various examples of my work. I have taught a number of workshops in New York, Oregon, and Massachusetts.

I produce approximately 120 bears a year all by myself. Some are one-of-a-kind, some are limited editions (20-25), and some open-ended. Most of my creations are sold retail.

The price of my creatures range from \$85 (3-1/2in {9cm}) to \$350 (24in {61cm}). The bears on all fours are \$300. Most of my bears are 14—18in (36—46cm) and sell for \$160 - \$200.

What truly gives me the most pleasure in bear making is the creative process itself. I love the research, the problem solving, the cut and paste — trial and error methods, converting minor disasters into positive contributing elements, operating at times on a right brain intuition basis only, and meeting the challenge of creating a three dimensional object from two dimensional forms.

There is a great thrill in watching the "bonding" that takes place between a bear and his new owner!

My hardest task is balancing real life (family responsibilities, community, etc.) with my work life. I believe half of my creative time is taken up with "business" requirements. Marketing takes away from the actual creative process. I am totally ignorant of "sales" skills. I love people and I hate selling.

BEAR MAKING HINTS: If your bear is on all fours and his hips are too fat perhaps he's eating too much honey! But, here's a way to "flatten him out:"

1. Trim away as much fur as possible on both the body of the bear directly under where the joint will be and trim the fur away on the inside of the limb directly over the joint.
2. Use as large a pair of washers as possible, still allowing for closure of the fabric.
3. Careful stuffing and shaping completes the process.

120. *Cornpone and His Prize Winning Pig, Sou-ee.* 1993. *Cornpone* and his prize winning pig, *Sou-ee* live near Mossy Log Woods in a quaint little farmhouse. Together they have implements appropriate to their occupations. *Cornpone* raises corn in many colors; *Sou-ee* enters beauty pageants. *Cornpone* is a fully jointed 16in (41cm) bear made of long, extra dense blonde mohair with an ultrasuede inset muzzle and hand-painted ultrasuede paw pads. *Sou-ee* is made of soft German plush, with ultrasuede ears and a fully jointed body. *Photograph by W. Donald Smith.*

Connie Tognoli
CONNIE'S BEARS AND BUNNIES

The first bears I made were in the 1970s for my young sons to use on their toy parachutes or helium balloons. They are still alive and well, but rather pathetic looking. The pattern was in a magazine on a grid to enlarge. I used it as it was printed, making the hand-stitched, felt bears about 2in (5cm).

I had been a doll artist for more than 20 years, designing original work in many different media. My first bears were created to enhance a Santa doll I made in 1985 called "Bearly Christmas." He delivers only Teddy Bears. It was a challenge to see how many different bears I could make. Santa carries 30 unique bears from 1—4in (3—10cm) in size. His companion is a larger roller bear on a leash that has baskets on his sides, filled with more bears, bear books, posters, and other bear articles.

Now I make more than 50 kinds of bears and am constantly creating different ones. Most are jointed 1—4in (3—10cm). I use velour, stretch velvet, and some mohair. In addition to the bears I originally created for the "Bearly Christmas" I make holiday bears (Santas, pumpkins, snowmen), story book (my personal favorite, Red Riding Hood), sewing bears, nurse bears, birthday bears, and roller bears. And these are just a few!

I am also interested in American Cloth Dolls. I've designed a number of dolls to use as accessories for one of my 20in (51cm) Santa Dolls to hold. All told, I make approximately 200 bears and 150 bunnies a year, along with the original dolls and other animals. I do all the design and sewing, but my husband Joe, does complementary woodwork for dolls and bears.

121. Connie Tognoli enjoys the creative challenge of making character dolls to add to her vast and wonderful bear and animal family line. Pictured is a Red Riding Hood and Wolf doll. *Photograph by J.W. Biller.*

I have a very wide range of items as well as prices. I make a tiny 1in (3cm) flat bear for $5. My Santa Doll with ten bears is $400. The average cost of a small 2-1/2in (6cm) bear is $25.

BEAR MAKING HINTS: Trace your patterns onto the fabric and sew the pieces before cutting them out. This enables you to sew the tiniest pieces much more easily.

122. *Bearly Christmas.* 1986. *Santa Doll.* 20in (51cm); hand-painted chalkware face and hands; cloth body; *Santa* is surrounded by 30 different handmade tiny teddies. The Roller bear is unjointed with two tiny baskets filled with little gifts and bears hanging from its back. *Photograph by J.F. Biller.*

62

Connie Tognoli
CONNIE'S BEARS AND BUNNIES

123. *Special Crayon Delivery.* 1995. An unjointed bear on all fours with metal wheels, pulls a wheeled crayon box full of brightly colored, velour, jointed miniature bears. Their tiny hats are made of crayon wrappers. The Flag reads: "Special Crayon — Delivery." The entire piece measures 4-1/2in (12cm) tall by 10in (25cm) long. One-of-a-kind. *Photograph by J. F. Biller.*

124. Julia Watada specializes in making tiny bear and bunny creations ranging from 5/8—3in (2—8cm).

Julia Watada
WATADA DESIGNS

Specializing in very limited edition bears, I have been making miniature bears (less than 3in [8cm]) since 1987. After dabbling in several different craft media (illustration, quilt-making, doll-making), I started bear-making with miniature Fimo® bears. I soon realized that quality bears were few and hard to find (and very expensive), so with a lifetime of sewing skills behind me, I set out to make high-quality sewn bears.

With a BS in Applied Art Design and Graphic Design concentration from Cal Polytechnic in San Luis Obispo, I have a full-time job in graphic design, but I manage to find time to design and create my bears and sell them at two shows a year.

I have won many awards at various shows. My bears sell for $85 and up; they are easily identified by the suede tag bearing my name and the date of the bear's creation.

I enjoy the challenge of coming up with new design ideas for my bears. The hardest task, I find, is the repetitive work involved in supplying many bears of the same design; nonetheless, I find making bears a welcome relaxation.

BEAR MAKING HINTS: Instead of cutting paper patterns for bear pieces, buy some duralene from a graphics store and make a stencil of pieces from it. The pattern is then durable and easy to hold.

125. (Bottom left) *Ballerina Bear.* 1989. 1-3/4in (5cm). (Top row left to right) *Dressed Holiday Bear.* 1992. 2in (5cm). *Dressed Bear.* 1995. 2in (5cm). *Mini Bo Bear.* 1990. 3in (8cm). *Stamp Size Teddy* (grouped with two tiny bunnies). 1995. 1-1/2in (4cm). *Blond Bear.* 1990. 3in (8cm). *Bear In Red Shirt.* 1994. 1-5/8in (4cm).

MaryAnn Wills
TEDDY BEARS WITH EXPRESSION

I traveled to my first bear show in Timonium, Maryland to exhibit my bears in the late eighties. My car was packed full; the sun was beginning to rise; I was feeling very unsure and ready to cry. I turned on the car radio and the theme from "Rocky" was playing. As I listened and drove, I felt taller and stronger and the "Rocky" spirit filled me. By the time I arrived at the show, I was READY. It was a wonderful experience and I felt so comfortable and at home. I knew without a doubt that this was for me.

My husband, Raymond Wills, inspired me to create my first bears. I always want others to feel the love I felt when I hugged a teddy. I do all the work myself:

126. It is the whimsical and appealing facial expression of Mary Ann Wills' bears that has earned her recognition in the bear world.

designing, creating, working on one piece from start to finish. My wonderful family does household chores so that I can "Bear."

I create mostly fully jointed, entirely original teddies and friends filled with love and soul. Most of my creations are mohair, hand-dyed from 4in (10cm) at $95 to 48in (122cm) at $995. When I do more than one of a bear, I give each individual expressions and make them in a variety of colors. To duplicate identically is not art to me.

BEAR MAKING HINTS:
1. Label your patterns. If you decide to make a change, make a new pattern piece and mark the date and why you decided to make the change (just in case you decide you don't want to change it or make less of a change).
2. Use different color paper for different size bear patterns to make it easier to keep the pieces together.

Janet Wilson
HANDMADE TREASURES

Ever since the day I could hold a crayon and a pair of scissors I have been creating one thing or the other. My grandmother taught me to use a sewing machine and I began making clothing for dolls as well as my grandmother and myself. Over the years, I've tried many different crafts. During the 80s, my husband Alex (who is also my partner) and I made and sold a variety of crafts, many of which we designed ourselves. Even though we had a lot of orders, there really wasn't any money in crafts. With a son preparing to enter college, I was forced to give up full-time crafting and take on a secretarial job for a local molding manufacturer. My favorite part of the job was designing displays and some drawing. The job lasted for four years and then my mother became ill.

I was looking for something to do and heard about Dickie Harrison and her wonderful miniature Teddy Bears. I am happiest when I am creating and the thought of becoming a Teddy Bear artist intrigued me. Two weeks after my mom passed away, I met Dickie and she opened my eyes to the wonderful world of collectible Teddy Bears. She sent me home to make my first pattern. Over the next month I took each of my new

127. Janet Wilson credits Teddy Bear artist Dickie Harrison for inspiring and helping her enter the Teddy Bear artist world.

Continued on page 65.

64

attempts down to her. She would critique my work, then I would go home to improve my pattern. Through sheer determination and joy, I managed to sell my first handful of miniature teddies at the 1990 Fall Teddy Bear Show in Baltimore, Maryland.

My bears are primarily miniature bears 1-1/8—3in (3—8cm). They are fully wire and disk jointed, predominantly made of upholstery velvet with ultra suede paw pads. Eyes are black onyx or glass beads. The faces are embroidered and totally hand-stitched. Most dressed bears average about $150. I make up to 200 bears and do about five shows a year.

Being a perfectionist, I start with the best bear I can make. Then, most of the bears are dressed. It is interesting that I collect mostly undressed bears, but I enjoy the challenge of dressing a mini-teddy and tend to put a great deal of detail into my work. The clothing is sewn, not glued to the bear. It might take me an entire day to just dress a bear. I also make many of their accessories.

I have had three TOBY® nominations and three Golden Teddy nominations. I received a Golden Teddy Award in 1993 for *Wynken, Blynken, and Nod.*

128. *Sprinkles.* 1994. 3in (8cm); upholstery velvet; black onyx bead eyes; fully jointed. Hand painted colored sprinkles applied to mohair. Handmade Fimo® ice cream cone. Hand-dyed silk ribbon bows. Limited edition of 35. *Photograph by Glen Taylor*

129. *Wynken, Blynken,* and *Nod.* 1993. 2-3/8in (6cm); upholstery velvet; glass bead eyes; fully jointed bodies; hand-painted wooden shoe; fabric sail; nightshirts and hats made of antique linen, hankies decorated with pearl buttons. Limited edition of 6. 1993 Golden Teddy Award winner. *Photograph by Glen Taylor.*

Joyce Yates
BEARLY VICTORIAN

130. Joyce Yates proudly stands with members of her "Bearly Victorian" family creations. (Top row left to right) *Baby Christina,* 1994. *Lady Thornbeary.* 1995. *Gwendolyn Fareday,* 1994. In the forefront are fully jointed mohair bears in sizes 4-1/2—9in (12—23cm) accessorized with boas and adorable hats lavishly trimmed with feathers, silk roses, ribbons and bows.

My dream was always to be creative and artistic and to be self-employed. My bears grew out of these desires. I also have always felt inspired to transform wonderful fabric and materials into an object that would bring pleasure to others as well. In the past, I have studied clothing construction, pattern drafting, Japanese floral arrangement, pottery, and silk ribbon embroidery. I have always been involved with a "hands-on" art project in one form or another. I am completely self-taught in bear design and construction.

My bears are my original designs. I make about 200 a year. They range in size from 7/8— 20in (2—51cm); they are priced from $55 to $225, depending on size and materials. My bears are styled and accessorized with a Victorian and Vintage theme. Color blending and coordinating is a very important aspect of my designs. I try to include a touch of whimsy in my work, particularly when creating miniatures. I also design and sew dresses and hats for my bears and sometimes costume them with Vintage materials.

I exhibit at approximately 12 shows — primarily Teddy Bear and miniature shows — a year.

Presently I work alone with the emotional and moral support of my husband, Bill, daughter, Alicia and faithful dog, Patrick. I have plans to increase my inventory and to achieve this goal, I need to have someone assist me with the routine tasks.

Barbara Zimmerman
ZIMM'S BEARS & HARES

My real Teddy Bear is my husband, Ted. I met him when I was a widow with small children. Early in our relationship I asked him what happened to his childhood Teddy Bear. When he replied, "I never had one," I decided no man named Teddy should ever go through life without a Teddy Bear.

So, since 1982, I have been designing bears and several years ago added Twirling Bears, Pandas, and other animals to my repertoire. I like traditional bears and design mine with long legs and big feet. They are all fully jointed. Personally, I like quality fur bears, so I seldom dress a bear. When I do, I usually remake vintage clothing.

My husband, Ted, and I also created a wooden toy for all ages which is also been marketed successfully. Ted helps me to make all things possible — cuts, stuffs, tightens joints, gives me understanding, and encouragement and is with me at all shows.

It was my daughter Lisa who insisted that I branch out from craft shows and exhibit at my first exclusive Teddy Bear Show in 1993. Now I do four or five shows a year.

BEAR MAKING HINTS: Place a smaller cotter pin through the head of the cotter pin you plan to put through the disk Curl ends of smaller pin. This will keep you from pulling the cotter pin through the disk when you tighten the joint.

131. Barbara Zimmerman with one of her favorite 1995 bear creations *Razzamatazz. Photograph by Judy York.*

132. (Left) *Abbot.* 1995. 10-1/2in (27cm); white feather fluff mohair; German black glass eyes; fully jointed. (Right) *Dan Dee.* 1995. 24in (61cm); extra dense blue curly mohair; German black glass eyes; fully jointed. *Photograph by Judy York.*

67

Marie Zimmermann
PAW QUETTE BEARS

133. According to Marie Zimmermann the rewards of bear making come from her collectors that appreciate her talents when they love her bears and give them good homes.

134. *Cherry Blossom.* 1995. 16in (41cm); swirly mauve and creme mohair; glass eyes; fully jointed.

I've been sewing practically since I can remember. My mother sewed everything when I was young and I always insisted on "helping" her. Now she helps me by doing all my pin basting. I also have a lady who designs and hand knits all of the sweaters and knitted lace dresses. Otherwise, all my work is done by me.

I majored in English and Speech with a theater emphasis my first time through college. My dream was to become a famous costume designer. Several years later I changed my major to Veterinary Technology. After graduation I ended up with a good mix of design and animal anatomy — a good background for bear making, don't you think?

I have two basic styles with variations in both which I like. One is what I call the "Classic Paw Quette," the style with the "adopt-me-puppy" look; the other, developed in 1993, is the Antique Paw Quette, with hump back, long, thin arms and snout, and over-sized feet. Many have a Victorian look.

I work more hours than I ever worked before in my life and have been doing this for almost six years. I look forward to every day, and produce happily and systematically approximately 320 bears per year. I haven't "burned out" yet. What a great thing to do for a living!

Most of my sales are retail. I do about 15 shows and signings a year. Paw Quette bears range from 11—34in (28—86cm) and sell for $95 to $475 and up. My bears are increasingly one-of-a-kind, still some open-ended and approximately three limited editions per year.

I love what I do. Life is an adventure and always full of changes.

BEAR MAKING HINTS:
1. Style develops over time. It comes from within. It gives your work soul, life, character. It is the part of the bear that appeals to the collector and the maker. It should be a continuing process that hopefully does not end.
2. Technique is also developed, but it can be learned.

68

135. Linda Benson prides herself in creating and producing her bears entirely on her own. However, she feels at times it would be wonderful to have help with the cutting and stuffing!

Linda Benson
BENSON BEARS

I thought I was 16 when I made my first bear. I had found a book of patterns while browsing in the library and thought a bear would be a pleasing thing to make. Well, who can stop at just one! But my sister insists that I got started even earlier when I was nine and made a bear from old curtain material. Who knows!

One of my first bears was made from a very shaggy, yellow bath mat; he wasn't very well jointed and fell apart when a dog got hold of him.

As you can see, I know bearmaking materials often show up unexpectedly and aren't necessarily expensive. After you've been making bears for a while you learn to "see" bears in all sorts of things. When I first started making bears there was very little in the way of quality fabrics available in Australia. Charity shops were a good source of fake fur. These days, though, I use almost nothing but mohair because it gives the most pleasing results. Perhaps my background in textiles (Diploma of Fine Art) aids me in developing in the area of material selection.

Until recently I haven't been in a position to pursue bearmaking to the extent I do now. My twin children are less dependant on my time, so I hope to enter more competitions and do some teaching or workshops in the future.

Currently I make at least a bear a day. They are basically old-fashioned, handcrafted, high quality originals, measuring 3/4—20in (2—51cm). My really tiny bears are used as accessories and aren't generally sold separately. I charge from around $50 to $300 (AUST) (approximately $39 to $235) depending on the size.

BEAR MAKING HINTS: On larger bears, use a 4in (10cm) doll needle for embroidering noses; they're easy to manipulate and ensure snug and even stitches.

136. *Three brothers.* 1995. 17in (43cm); honey-colored English mohair; old wooden boot button eyes; fully jointed. Pellet filled body with buckshot added for weight.

69

Samantha Fredericks
BLISS TOYS

My first Limited Edition was a very small felt penguin that lives in a fabric covered matchbox with a pillow, sheets, and blankets. I was eight when I made him and four others like him, including one for the mother of my best friend. She tells me she still has it displayed in her bedroom.

My interest in bear collecting first emerged during a backpacking trip around Germany and Europe with my Teddy Bear. He collected a few friends along the way and continued his obsession for amassing furry four legged friends once we came home. On a camping trip a year later, he hurled himself into a raging river and after 25 years of valuable service, ran away to start a feral bear colony in the mountains. I vowed to make thousands in his likeness, so that his memory would live on. I now work full time designing and creating bears and animals.

I began Bliss Toys in 1992. Until December 1994 I kept my full time job in marketing, but then, at the age of 29, I resigned to follow my heart, indulge my creativity, and further develop myself as a bear and animal artist. To promote my fledgling bear business, I advertise in *Bear Facts Review, Dolls, Bears & Collectibles, Teddy Bear and Friends®*, and *Hugglets*. I sell retail, wholesale, through reps, and occasionally deal with private orders.

I currently produce approximately 350—400 bears a year and am the only full time worker at Bliss Toys. My mother does all of the cutting, my father makes discs for joints and exotic props for shows, my brother is Chief Stuffer, and my sister and another friend are my two Sales Managers. I handle all other aspects of the business, including hand dying of fabrics. Each bear and animal is completely original.

Bliss Toys is best known in Australia for childsafe Limited Edition

137. Samantha Fredericks with three of her unique bear creations. (Left to right) *Delores.* 1995. 10in (25cm). *Tim Lion.* 1995. 11in (28cm). *Carl.* 1995. 13in (33cm). All animals portray examples of Samantha's typical waxed nose feature. They are identified with an oval "Bliss B Toys" label stitched onto the foot or worn as a hang tag around the neck.

bears. However, I recently introduced a range of 16 Special Edition Animals, which is my best work to date and has been an outstanding success. All Bliss Toys bears and animals have fine mohair coats and are fully jointed. The Special Edition bears and animals feature hand painted detailing, stencilled paw pads, glass, and antique shoe button eyes and pellet filled tummies. The Limited Edition bears are more traditional in their designs although some of them have hand dyed mohair coats in vibrant colors. My bears are characterized by unusual body designs and facial expressions. I now have polar bears, pandas, fat bears with three piece bodies, and a very popular skinny bear who has just emerged from hibernation. They range in cost and size from $115 (AUST) (approximately $87) for a little 7in (18cm) bear to $375 (AUST) (approximately $284) for an 18in (46cm) Polar Bear.

My ultimate goal is for Bliss Toys to be known both in Australia and around the world as a proud Australian producer of both fine quality collectible artist pieces and toys for children and adults of all ages. Although my bears are currently adopted by collectors, they are intended to be strong enough to withstand a lifetime of human experience as well as enjoy the company of other artist bears in a collection.

BEAR MAKING HINTS: In order to make even feet paw pads, mark a center line down the inside length of the paw pad and also mark the toe and heel extremes of the leg. Then match up and pin the marks so that the pad is stretched evenly in both directions.

138. (Left) *Adelaide.* 1995. 10in (25cm); swirly golden mohair; antique shoe button eyes; suede paw pads; fully jointed; cotton, polyfill and pellet stuffed torso. (Center) *Bonnie.* 1995. 10in (25cm); alfonzo red mohair; antique shoe button eyes; suede paw pads; fully jointed; cotton polyfill and pellet stuffed torso. (Right) *Delores.* 1995. 10in (25cm); sky blue mohair; antique shoe button eyes; suede paw pads; fully jointed; cotton, polyfill and pellet stuffed torso. All bears have hand painted brown detailing on snout, ears, and paws and a waxed nose.

Ronwyn Graham
BAMBINI DESIGN

139. Involved in reproduction doll making for approximately seven years, Ronwyn Graham's interest in teddy bears began in 1992. During the last 18 months she has been concentrating on creating miniature bears under 3-1/8in (5cm) tall.

140. *Magician.* 1993. 3-3/8in (9cm); pale silvery gray upholstery fabric; black onyx eyes; fully jointed. Ultrasuede top hat and tails, bunny peeping out of hat, dove on ring. Limited edition of 15. 1993 TOBY® nominee.

Perhaps it is no surprise that I would turn to making miniature bears after an avid interest in the miniature art of Bonsai. My concentration on these tiny creatures has brought me a number of First Awards and two Best in Section awards at shows. I received a TOBY® nomination for my miniature *Magician* in 1993 and another one for *Me and my Friends* in 1995. The later measure in at 5—7in (13—18cm) and are created from German mohair.

Most of my little bears are in editions of 15. The rest are open, but rarely exceed 15 to 20. The open bears are numbered so that if a collector wants to know 12 months down the track how many were produced I can tell them.

Miniature bears made from upholstery fabric retail between $75—$215 (AUST) (approximately $58—$168). Larger mohair and alpaca bears range between $130 to $380 (AUST) (approximately $99—$288).

I enjoy selling directly to collectors. I really enjoy attending shows where I can talk with new and old collectors who share my love of Teddy Bears.

71

161. (Left) *Kanga.* 1993. 12in (31cm); white mohair; glass eyes; fully jointed. Limited edition of 5. (Right) *B.B. Bear.* 1995. 10in (25cm); honey colored mohair; glass eyes; fully jointed. Bear is wearing the keys, friendship bracelet, name tag (wooden) and beads which represent different levels students complete during the "earth awareness" campaign which takes place at the College Briony's son attends.

162. *Fiske.* 1995. 10in (25cm); Barramundi fish skin; glass eyes; fully jointed. All bears are completely hand stitched, and made from hand dyed Barramundi fish skin. "Barramundi" is an Aboriginal word.

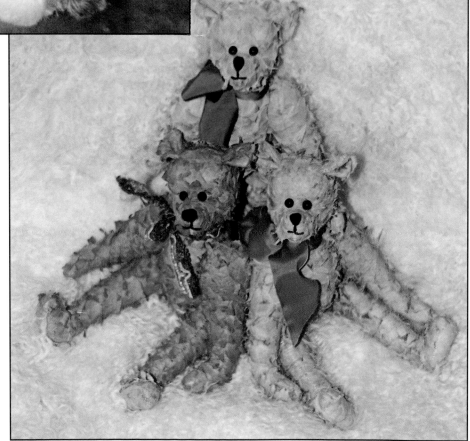

82

Debbie Sargentson
NOSTALGIA BEARS-AUSTRALIA

Nostalgia bears are known for their old world appearance and the addition of antique or collectible accessories. They are predominantly recognized by their large ears, long limbs, and the style of nose I create for each bear. A small number of truly special bears are commissioned each year by private collectors with each bear standing at least 29in (74cm) and elaborately costumed to the finest detail.

Some of the commissioned bears I have made are Phantom of the Opera and a Russian princess in full beaded silk ball gown. Some of these can cost up to $2,000 (AUST) (approximately $1514) depending on the size, costuming, and accessories used. Most prices start at $275 (AUST) (approximately $208). Nostalgia bears start in size from 9in (23cm), however the majority of designs average approximately 15—17in (36—43cm).

Marketing my bears is an opportunity to merge my business and management skills from my previous corporate jobs with my role as a bear artist. Whilst I am truly passionate about creating my bears, I believe it takes a combination of business and art skills to be truly successful.

Nostalgia bears are available through a select number of retailers in Melbourne and Perth in Australia. Collectors can also purchase my bears directly from me through custom orders or via the four or five Teddy Bear shows I attend throughout Australia each year. Last year I even attended Linda's Teddy Bear show in California.

I have to thank my mum for the inspiration to create bears. She had been making bears for herself for a couple of years. This, coupled with my desire to return to a life long interest in needlework gave me the courage I needed to design a pattern to make my first bear in May 1993.

These days my hardest task is finding the time to bring all of my ideas to life. I always seem to have five or six new ideas in my head and never enough time to create them. This is why I'm quite sure I'll be making bears for many years to come!

163. Debbie Sargentson never dreamed that after only three weeks of bear making she would win a blue ribbon for her work and be approached by three retail bear shops proposing to represent her work. From this beginning, her Nostalgia Bears have grown into a full time passion and business.

164. *Marmaduke and Marmaduke Junior.* 1994. *Marmaduke.* 24in (61cm); *Marmaduke Junior.* 10in (25cm); cinnamon colored German dense mohair; black glass eyes; fully jointed. *Marmaduke* represents Debbie's interpretation of a Grizzly type bear. His long limbs, forest green suede paws, quizzical expression, larger ears, and nose design create this unique looking new design. *Marmaduke* wears his gold name tag. *Marmaduke Junior* is a Bear backpack resting on *Marmaduke's* back with suede ties and he carries an old brass compass and map so the pair do not get lost when traveling through the woods at night. Limited edition of 75.

83

Amanda Heugh

183. Most of Amanda Heugh's unique one-of-a-kind character bears are in small editions with Welsh names, many of which reflect the mountains or valleys of their native land. They embody the warmth and friendship of the Welsh culture.

From the mountains and valleys of the spectacular Snowdonia National Park, my bears travel the world as ambassadors of Wales. They embody the warmth and friendship of the Welsh culture, radiating happiness and tranquility to all those who live with them.

The idea of making bears came from a re-location to one of the most beautiful parts of Wales. "Craggy" bears, oozing with personality, are named after natural wonders like mountains and valleys; historical Character Bears are named after people like Llywelyn and Owain; and the more delicate little bears are named after Tylwyth Teg (Welsh Fairies). They are made from only the best mohair, alpaca, and wool, with wool felt/suede for paws and pads, old-fashioned hardboard joints, glass or old boot-button eyes, and filled with high quality wadding and polyethylene pellets.

My hardest task is making sure that my bears are always seen at their best; this is especially hard when displayed in shops and squashed onto shelves. Being mostly soft and pellet filled, they do not travel well and always need a lot of Tender Loving Care when they reach their destination.

I do not draw, but actually design new bears in my head, using fabric and color as my basis, and starting with the bear's name and its derivation. For instance, Ogwen, the name of which is actually a lake below the mountain Tryfan, gave me an image of a little, old, whiskery lady wrapped in a shawl. And that's how she was born.

I am very proud to be named the Runner-up to New Artist of the Year 1994 in my first year at the British Bear Artist Awards held at Croydon by *Teddy Bear Times*. I have also been awarded Business Woman of 1994 for North West Wales, an award for women running small businesses.

I make approximately 450 bears a year, and exhibit at 12 fairs a year, about one a month. You can also find my bears in retail shops in the UK and abroad. I also run a Mail Order business.

I am committed to using only the best materials that I can afford. I never rush. Each bear is a work of art in itself.

BEAR MAKING HINTS:
1. Balance both home and work life. Keep a daily appointment diary and stick to it!
2. Close the door at the end of the work day, so you can relax without the pressure of work staring you in the face.

184. (Left to right) *Fircone.* 1994. 11in (28cm); warm colored cinnamon striped distressed mohair; black glass eyes; fully jointed; pellet and wadding stuffing. Limited edition of 25. *Geraint.* 1993. 16in (41cm); rich cinnamon colored distressed mohair; black glass eyes; fully jointed; pellet and wadding stuffing; wrinkled tummy and forehead; pronounced hump on back. Limited edition of 15. *Hendre.* 1995. 19-1/2in (50cm); color blended (blond tones) distressed mohair; black glass eyes; fully jointed; pellet and wadding stuffing. Limited edition of 6. *Oliwen.* 1993. 14in (36cm); pale golden colored weave distressed mohair; black glass eyes; fully jointed; pellet and wadding stuffing. Limited edition of 15.

185. Jill Hussey credits the American Teddy Bear artists for her inspiration and influence in creating her own bear designs.

To be honest, lately I have had trouble keeping up with the demand for my bears. They have really taken off here and the shops are selling them as quickly as they come in! I am told my bears are highly individualistic and great emphasis is placed on each expression of personality.

I work on my own, usually twelve hours a day. But my husband does give me a hand with the stuffing. I've only been making bears for a little over a year now, but last year produced 500 of them. They are made of mohair and come in sizes of 7in (18cm), 14in (36cm), and 25in (64cm).

I like to see each new bear come to life as I finish the face. They are all real to me and tell me how they wish to look. (Honestly sometimes the most difficult task in this endeavor is keeping my overactive imagination in check.) It is wonderful to see the pleasure bears bring to other people. Most folks either laugh at the bear's whimsical expressions or want to comfort the sad ones!

BEAR SELLING TIPS:
1. Price bears carefully and take into account all the hidden costs that arise. When selling bears through shops, mail order or fairs, make sure your prices are comparable to those of other artist bears.
2. Always be friendly, not aggressive in your selling manner, and treat people to a smile.

186. *Tattered and Torn.* This enchanting pair was a shop exclusive produced in a limited edition of 12.

93

Michaela Parnell
MICHA BEARS

I am German. When I was in England with my English husband on holiday in 1991 I fell in love with a 1-1/2in (4cm) bear at the toy store, "Hamley's" in London. Two years later I was selling my small, happy mohair bears with full figures to the general public. Now I make 150—200 bears a year. Most of my sales are through selected shops and bear fairs. My one-of-a-kind and limited editions (20—25 bears) all have a sewn-in label which identifies me as the sole maker. It says "Exclusive Designs by Micha Bears."

All of my bears are undressed, but usually hold something like a miniature bear, Gollie, pet, or muff.

Recently, I was deeply touched by a collector who started to buy my bears after her father died. She told me that my bears had given her much comfort because of their happy natures and smiling faces. Now she has about 60 of my bears!

BEAR MAKING HINTS:
1. When using silk ribbons on miniature bears, use a little hair spray on the finished bow. It stops it from fraying and keeps it in nice shape.
2. If you have pets, keep your needles on a pincushion, safe in a box all the time. (Cats especially love to play with needle and thread).

192. The happy-looking expression of Michaela Parnell's bears have brought pleasure to many people in need of comfort.

Louise Peers

Almost as soon as Linda Mullins asked me to become part of this book, I won an award at the British Bear Artist Awards '95! My *Morris Teds* were selected for the best in the Miniature Bears group 5in (13cm) and under. This was my first official award.

Before specializing in miniature bears, I made a few large bears and before that soft toys of all types, mainly aiming at the children's market. Today I mainly create miniature bears 1-1/2—3-1/2in (4—9cm) in limited editions of under ten.

Even though it is difficult to accomplish many tasks when you have two small children to look after (Sophie and Nicholas), I manage to produce between 200—250 bears a year and exhibit at six or seven shows.

It never ceases to surprise me how many people love and collect bears. I recently discovered that a mum whose son is in my daughter's class at school (and lives a mile away) recently bought one of my bears whilst on holiday in Brighton some 260 miles away. She didn't even realize that I made bears!

193. Louise Peers proudly poses with her one-of-a-kind award winning creation *Morris Teds.* This exquisite piece won the miniature bear category (5in[13cm] and under) award in the 1995 British Bear Artist Competition. Each bear is 2-1/2in (6cm) tall dressed to represent Morris dancers.

BEAR MAKING HINTS: To make a silk ribbon flower, cut 2in (5cm) narrow silk ribbon, fray check ends to seal. When dry, run a tiny gathering thread along the top edge and pull-up tight and knot off; this forms a ruffled circle; you can the add a seed bead for the center of the flower. You can then make a few and join together for a garland for your tiny bear to wear.

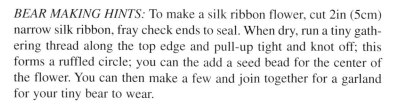

194. (Left) *Easter Parade.* 1995. 2-1/2in (6cm); white head and paws; blue body; upholstery fabric; onyx bead and eyes; fully jointed; Easter bonnet decorated with chicks; basket with foil eggs. One-of-a-kind. *Fizzy.* 1995. 2in (5cm); pink head and torso, blue arms and legs; upholstery fabric; onyx bead eyes; fully jointed; hand painted feather butterfly wings. One-of-a-kind. Small jointed bear in center with bunny ears is 1-1/2in (4cm) tall.

96

Katherine R. Rabjohn
CALICO BEARS

I love a challenge. My bears have big noses and quite quirky faces with loads of character. They come in little calico bags made by my husband Robert who we call "The Bag Man."

It was Robert who really got me into bear making. I had been ill and had a month off work. Robert bought me a miniature kit. I made it; threw away the pattern and started designing my own. Even though I had previously made a big bear named "Blossom" the year before (wearing an exact replica of my wedding dress), it was the miniatures that my good friends from "Growlies" convinced me were good enough to sell. And Karl, from Theodore's Bear Emporium, continually encourages me to do bigger and better things.

I think the thing that has brought me the most pleasure was when I was asked to do a bride and groom as a surprise for the top of a wedding cake. It took months of planning as I copied the wedding dress. The groom was in full Scottish dress. I even managed to copy the tartan. But the end product was worth it and the bride was thrilled.

The most important thing for me is the designing and creating of bears. If I sell them it is an added bonus. I have a very hectic life style, working full-time as a receptionist in an advertising agency, singing in a band, and mothering a wonderful baby boy named Jordan Charlie. You can see why I tend not to do many shows as I can't really make enough bears. They are sold as fast as I can make them!

BEAR MAKING HINTS:
Here's how to keep ends of thread neat and eliminate knots when sewing miniatures: Use the longest piece of quilting thread (because it doesn't tangle) you feel you can work with; one piece of thread per body part works well; when you have finished stuffing the head (for example) attach a long piece of thread to the opening at the bottom of the head; close the opening: pass the needle up to the first ear, sew on; then pass over to the other ear and then back down to under the head. DO NOT CUT THIS OFF. You may need it for face sculpturing later. Do this with every color thread you are using. Then, when you are sure all sewing has been completed, sew up the threads under the head. When the head is attached the ends will be hidden. The same applies to the other body parts. For example, sew up the arms; leave the thread hanging; turn and stuff the arm; then rethread the cotton and sew up the opening; pass the thread to the front of the arm; pull as tight as possible and snip close to the body; then let go. The end of the thread will disappear inside, eliminating any knots or ends of thread.

195. Katherine Rabjohn says she was inspired to make Teddy Bears from her appreciation of the talented artists' work around the world. Her friends' ongoing encouragement drives her to make even better things!

196. *Friends of Fur.* 1994. 2-1/2in (6cm); light beige upholstery velvet; glass eyes; fully jointed. The bear affectionately holds a 1in (3cm) white spaniel pup. Limited edition of 10 (pairs).

197. Teresa Rowe and her magnificent one-of-a-kind bear, *The Honey Thief,* make a beautiful pair. Crafted in soft golden mohair, the bear has quilted and padded paws with handmade claws. *Photograph by Robert Taylor Studio.*

198. Occupying the center of this cute scene is *Baggins and Boo Boo Jack-In-A-Box.* Produced in 1995, the bear (dressed as a clown) is 9in (23cm), mohair, fully jointed with glass eyes. His face is hand embroidered. He comes with his own monkey. The wooden box is handpainted to enhance the theme. A working Jack-in-the-box movement. Surrounding the box are (top left) *Pee-Wee,* (top right) *Billy Bramley,* (bottom left) *Rambling Rose,* (bottom right) *Tommy Tadpole. Photograph by Robert Taylor Studio.*

I was inspired to make bears when I left my job to have my second child. I found that the bears I liked best were out of my price range and so, having a creative background, I decided to try and make my own. My nearest bear shop, "Bear with Us" in Lichfield was very encouraging and said they would be interested to see what I made. My first commercial bear was "Mr. Bumble and the Bee," a limited edition of ten. I sold him not only to "Bear with Us", but to other shops as well. And so began "Waifs & Strays."

I have always created character bears. They are 9—12in (23—31cm) mainly dressed, as it gives me greater scope for originality and development in both features and clothing. One of the most enjoyable parts of creating a new character is the choosing and coordinating of all the various fabrics and accessories. I do create some undressed bears, although I like to think I make them a little different from the "norm" with padded paws and shaped arms and legs.

I make only 100 to 150 bears a year (about three bears a week), believing in quality and not quantity. Most of my bears are in editions of 20 or less. I also enjoy creating one-of-a-kind bears, particularly special commission where I can really "go to town" in terms of the time and amount of detail put into them. I spend many hours creating a single bear; this is not the best way to make a fortune, I know, but that isn't the main objective for me.

My bears are not identified by one particular look, as I change my patterns and techniques often. They're more identifiable by their character, workmanship, attention to fine detail, and the use of fabrics. If I am unable to find a particular small accessory needed to complete a character (buttons, claws, even spiders), I make it myself.

I have been making bears since 1992 and have been fairly successful in the British Bear Artist Awards with three runners up. I hope to win this year!

BEAR MAKING HINTS:
1. To stuff a bear firmly and evenly, use a plastic chopping board with shallow holes drilled into one side. Rest the board on your knee and place your stick into a hole on the board to stop it from flipping. This then leaves both hands free to push the stuffing into the body parts.
2. Foot pads are very important to the look of a bear and should be uniform in appearance. To achieve perfect paws every time, always hand sew them. It takes longer, but it is worth it.
3. When making an edition of bears, it is easier to achieve a uniform look by keeping a note of measurements for such things as eye position, nose dimensions, ear positions and joint settings.
4. When stock needs replenishing, write it down straight away. It's so easy to forget until you come to the stage when you finally run out of something!

Sandra Wickenden
WICKENDEN BEARS

199

When I was diagnosed with multiple sclerosis, some doors were closed. Others opened. Particularly the doors to making my hobby what it is today...a very rewarding and enjoyable pastime which happily works around my health and family situation.

I am inspired by tradition. I love antiques from the Victorian/Edwardian eras, so it is not surprising that I am inspired by the early Edwardian Teddy Bears, especially those of Steiff. I not only create bears to capture this rich tradition but aim to capture the genre with components such as pure mohair, thick wool felt pads and old boot buttons, when I can get them. All of my bears are stuffed with wood wool, hoping to recreate the comfort and love which oozes out of old filled bears. Getting a bear out of my head and into reality for a cuddle is one of my greatest pleasures.

Since I design and make all my bears myself, my production is limited — my objective is quality, not quantity. I am fortunate that my bears are not our livelihood and I can keep that objective. Predominantly "one-offs" and small editions suit my limited output. Some are sold through wonderful outlets in the U.K., U.S.A., Germany, and Japan. I only do five shows a year, comprising of the *Hugglets* Festivals and *Teddy Bear Times* Fairs.

You can tell my bears because each one has a "w" for Wickenden embroidered as claws on all four paw pads.

BEAR MAKING HINTS: Store wood wool in big polythane bags to prevent from drying out; be sure to puncture the bags with small holes to prevent sweating.

Top to Bottom: **199.** Sandra Wickenden desired to personally create a Teddy Bear as an heirloom for her daughters to treasure. That started her on a new path in her life that she never looks back on. For Sandra bearmaking is a very rewarding and enjoyable pastime which she happily works around her family life. *Photograph by Eric Hilton.*

200. (Left) *Bear Cub.* 1995. 20in (51cm); entire bear made from an antique fur coat; glass eyes; stationary arms and legs; swivel head; wood shavings and wool stuffing; free standing; sculpted nose and claws. Depicts a real bear. One-of-a-kind. (Right) *Bruin.* 1994. 13in (33cm) tall by 17in (43cm) long; honey colored German mohair; Victorian glass waistcoat buttons; stationary legs; swivel head; wood shavings and wool stuffing; steel frame encased in bear's body. One-of-a-kind. *Photograph by Eric Hilton.*

200

Carolyn Willis

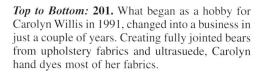

I was inspired to make miniature bears by my two fold love of Teddy Bears and anything miniature. I still have my two childhood straw-filled bears and am fascinated by tiny antique perfume bottles and watches from the 1930s which have tiny faces.

I create fully-jointed miniature bears from upholstery fabrics and ultra-suede, using various fillings such as polyester and steel ballbearings. I always use glass eyes and hand-dye most of the fabrics. I also design and produce kits.

I began making bears for sale in 1993. Perhaps the most interesting commission so far was to make a bear of my choice for a couple on their Silver Wedding Anniversary. The bear traveled along with them (in an un-opened box) to Venice where they were celebrating. They chose to wait until the big day before opening him. I was very honored, but a little apprehensive at the responsibility. It was with some considerable relief that I learned they were very happy with their new friend.

BEAR MAKING HINTS:
1. When cutting out limbs, check every corresponding piece to make sure they are exactly the same size.
2. Before jointing, find correct placement of limbs by temporarily attaching with pins. This is useful in making a bear sit or stand.
3. Sculpt the face by making eye sockets before attaching eyes; take a stitch at each eye position then tie off ends thorough neck opening, pulling hard to form two indentations.

201

Top to Bottom: **201.** What began as a hobby for Carolyn Willis in 1991, changed into a business in just a couple of years. Creating fully jointed bears from upholstery fabrics and ultrasuede, Carolyn hand dyes most of her fabrics.

202. *Genie on Magic Carpet.* 1994. 2-1/2in (6cm); white upholstery fabric; glass eyes; fully jointed; Indian silk clothes; glass beads individually hand sewn onto outfit; ultrasuede shoes; handpainted carpet. One-of-a-kind. Winner of the British Bear Artist Awards 1994. *Photograph by Huw Meredith.*

202

100

Patricia Gye
WAYFARER BEARS

I am in love with my bears and find it especially difficult to part with them. It is so hard to put a monetary value on them!

My bears, which are usually naked except for perhaps a hat, vest, shoes, collar or tie, are fully jointed, mostly traditional teddies. They range in size from 7—36in (18—91cm) and in price from Canadian $114 to $1060 (approximately $85 to $795), depending on the fabric length and type of pile, since this affects the amount of clipping required.

You can see it's one of my bears by the ultra suede "tush tag," which says Wayfarer Bears by Patricia. In addition to the tag sewn into his back seam, WB is written on his right heel and he has a hang tag bearing my logo, name, address, and details of materials.

Even though my wretched arthritis gets in the way sometimes, I do every bit of my creations myself, producing about 200 bears a year and attending five or six shows annually. I also sell by mail order and from my studio. I do happen to sell wholesale to a very, very few shops.

Over the years I have received quite a number of ribbons at Teddy Bear conventions. Two years running, I was presented with a hand carved glass plaque from the 1993 and 1994 Bear Fair conventions in Calgary and Alberta, Canada. I have been published in the a number of magazines and journals as well.

BEAR MAKING HINTS: Remember that the face is everything! Take time with them. Mark positions of the nose, eyes, and ears with pins, or even waterproof pens, before you commit yourself.

203

Top to Bottom: **203.** Patricia Gye, one of Canada's pioneer bear artists, believes the Canadian affinity for the woods and forestland shows in their bear art as well. A surprising percentage of the collectors tend to appreciate the more realistic bear, rather than the cutely attired bear. *Photograph by Della Garvin.*

204. (Left) *Otis.* 1995. 21in (53cm). (Right) *Otis Major.* 1995. 23in (58cm); both bears are made of beige curly German mohair; hand blown glass eyes; fully jointed. Stuffed with mixture of polyester fiberfill and nylon pellets to make them cuddly. Very intense facial expression. *Photograph by Della Garvin.*

204

101

Jane Perala
HEMER HOUSE DESIGNS

I was a potter for many years, with a line of functional and decorative stoneware. The pottery was put on hold while we built our present home, and I just didn't want to go back to it when the house was finished. We lived in a small travel trailer while the house was in the process of being built, and I had just enough room to set up a sewing machine, so I started sewing various dolls, rabbits, cows, and horses. I found there was a market for patterns of these original designs and started drafting the patterns and selling them through various fabric and craft shops and mail order magazines.

I took a trip to England and there were bears everywhere! So I added a teddy pattern to my line. Not all my bear designs are made into commercial patterns, some I keep just for me!

I am a very slow bear maker, and make between 150 to 175 mohair, fully jointed bears a year. I pay great attention to detail. For instance, I trim all the fur from the seam allowance on each piece before sewing. I always take great pains to make sure there is no trapped fur anywhere on the bear, both inside the seam and out.

When I design a new pattern, I usually give the first one a name and then nearly all the bears done in that pattern will have the same name.

When I finish a bear, I sit him or her on a chair in the living room and just watch him; all of a sudden they seem to come alive. It's truly magic.

BEAR MAKING HINTS: Ultra-suede stretches more one way than the other. For longer, thinner paws and foot pads, make sure you have the greater stretch from top to bottom. For fatter, wider paws and foot pads, have the greater stretch from side to side. Make sure both of the pads have the stretch in the same direction.

209. Jane Perala with her big bruin *Redfurred.* In addition to making wonderful bears Jane includes a large number of her sensitive soft sculptured dolls and animals in her catalog.

210. *Tasha.* 1995. 12-1/2in (32cm); pale cream colored curly mohair; glass eyes; fully jointed. Ultrasuede paws; cotton print sundress; straw hat and garden basket.

104

Cheryl Schmidt
IT BEARS REPEATING

I think my bears can safely be categorized in the "non-traditional" category. I like to tell people that although my bears are not the cuddly, snugly type, they are most happy to sit on a shelf and whisper quiet assurances or just bring smiles. They tend to have a very refined look, with a lot of definition and shape. My greatest pleasure comes from the people who enter my booth or approach my table and just kind of stare. Then, all of a sudden the corners of their mouth start to turn up and they break into a big grin. Sometimes, they apologize, as if they've offended me, but I always thank them. This is exactly the reaction I want!

I have yet to create a bear out of typical bear making fabrics. I sew a lot of vintage fabrics, recycled mohair, alpaca or llama coats, hats ...whatever. I am particularly proud of winning first place in the "Art from recycled materials" category at the Klondike Days Arts and Carts Fair in my home town of Edmonton, Alberta in 1993.

I believe that if you make a good bear, people will buy it. The possibilities are endless! I price my bears from $125 to $300. I produce between 100 to 150 bears a year. I use a lot of miniature bear making techniques to create my 7in (18cm) bears, so my hands are pretty sore at the end of the day.

I warned my husband Dwayne that once I started making bears that I would probably be hooked. Well, I was right. I made my first bear in 1990. Dwayne refers to these as the "peanut head" bears, since they kind of look like nuts with the addition of eyes. I made two of them as gifts for my new in-laws. I was very proud. In 1991, with the encouragement of the local doll store, I sold my first original designs. Sometimes I would like to track down every one of those wonderful people who bought one of those early bears and replace it. Some of the bears were truly awful.

Now I do the best quality of work that I can, all the time. My standards have changed as I have improved. Things that were so difficult at the beginning are much easier now and I never substitute quality for quantity.

BEAR MAKING BUSINESS HINTS:
1. Decide on your goals. Do you want to be the next "Steiff" or are you content to make a few bears every year to fund your "bear buying budget?"
2. Reevaluate your goals every year. What did you accomplish? (Be kind to yourself); What did you miss out on? (Be kinder to yourself).
3. Set realistic expectations for yourself. Customers appreciate realistic timetables for when to expect their bear and if you can deliver it earlier, great! Don't promise someone 25 bears in 14 days if you can only make one bear per day.
4. Be honest with yourself and the people that you do business with. If you goof up, admit it and move on. They may be angry at first, but in the end will respect the fact that you were honest.

211. Cheryl Schmidt enjoys the challenge of using materials different from the typical bear making fabrics. Vintage fabrics, hats, recycled mohair, alpaca and llama coats, all have endless possibilities for Cheryl when she creates her unique line of bears.

212. *Foam on the Range.* 1995. 7-1/2in (19cm); vintage custom dyed wool/mohair; glass eyes with suede eyelids; fully jointed; wire armature in arms and legs; 'soapy' chin of french knots and glass beading; handmade accessories. One-of-a-kind.

105

Chapter 9

DUTCH TEDDY BEAR ARTISTS

Ber Boom

I am slightly different than many of the other artists featured here in Linda Mullins' book. I actually paint Teddy Bears in water colors, colored pencil, and gouache. I began painting bears four years ago when my wife, Ingrid, manager of the bearshop "Akkerman Berengoed", encouraged me to do so.

Ever since I can remember, I've had a passion for drawing and painting. I am very fortunate to make a profession out of it and am now occupied as a teacher in presentation and design at a school for vocational training. After a day of teaching, I retreat to my studio.

Strictly speaking, my drawings are still lifes. My teddies remain in their role of playthings and I don't give them a human character. Frequently I place them in historic surroundings.

I produce about four or five paintings a year and recently won a first prize in a contest held by the magazine *Beer Bericht* and the Colour Box company. The award was for my "Roosevelt painting."

In the near future, I hope to put together a calendar with teddies for all seasons and design a teddy book with short stories and poems that go with my sketches.

218. Artist Ber Boom poses for this photograph in the garden of his home with examples of his outstanding paintings. Ber uses water colors, color pencil, and gouache to achieve these magnificent works of art.

Marjoleine Diemel-van Rijn
OLD TIME TEDDY'S

219. Seeing the beautiful mohair fabrics at her local doll show inspired Marjoleine Diemel-van Rijn to make a three-dimensional Teddy Bear. Today Marjoleine's "Old Time Teddy's" designs are sought after by collectors around the world.

220. (Left) *Ashley.* 17-1/2in (45cm); (Right) *Joshua.* 8-1/2in (22cm). Both bears are produced in silky golden mohair, with shoe button eyes and fully jointed bodies. Limited edition of 15 each.

It is a very international world. My bears live in Holland, Germany, Japan, Moscow, Canada, the U.S.A., England, Belgium, and Australia. It is wonderful to get letters from all over the world!

I was inspired to make bears when I saw a beautiful bear from Bo Bears in England. It was made by Stacey Lee Terry. Soon after, I was at a doll show and discovered several fabrics from which to make Teddy Bears. In January 1991 I made my first bear. By the following May I was making more of them.

Now I make 200 bears a year and do about 12 shows. My bears are mainly in two shops in the Netherlands and one in Germany. They vary in size from 8-1/2—25-1/2in (22—65cm) and are priced from $115 to $375.

People say they know my bears by their distinctive faces. The bears are antique styled, very much like the early Steiff bears. I do make and design the bears all by myself and there are three women who knit underwear and sweaters for them.

In 1992, just a year after my bear making began, I won two prizes: First prize at a Teddy Bear contest in The Hague and another won at a contest further south. You can see examples of my work published in *Teddy Bear and Friends*®, *Teddy Bear Times*, *Hugglets*, and *De Teddy Bear en Beerbericht*.

Jane Humme
JANE HUMME ORIGINAL BEARS

I was an avid collector of antique dolls and visited antique doll and toy shows frequently. There were so many lovely bears for sale, but the ones I liked the most were so expensive. Since my Auntie Elisabeth taught me how to knit, I have never stopped doing all sorts of crafts, so it was, of course, a challenge for me to try to make my own bear! It was a traditional bear and turned out well enough for me to start selling bears the next year, 1989.

When I make a bear larger than 6in (15cm) it is marked with a label sewn into the left side of the body. On smaller bears, I embroider my initials "JH" with red yard.

In 1993, visitors to the annual doll and Teddy Bear fair in Rotterdam selected one of my bears for the Publieksprijs award. I was extremely pleased since nearly 18,000 people see 85 bear artists and even more doll artists in two days.

I make small limited editions, but I prefer to make one-of-a-kind creations. My father makes the joints for the 125 bears I make a year.

Every time I make a bear it is exciting to see the results. Although I find stuffing with woodwool is quite devastating to my shoulders and wrists, I can't stop myself from buying more and more lovely materials to work with, even though I have plenty at home.

BEAR MAKING HINTS: In making an ear, sew the underside of the ear together leaving a small opening for turning. Clip off the corners before turning so you won't have thick lumps in the corners.

221. Jane Humme with her bears *Dominic* (left) and *Thomas* (right). Jane hand crafted both bears in 1995 from the finest quality mohair. Dominic wears an antique bell from a harness of a Friesian horse. *Photograph by Ad Roos.*

222. (Left) *Lotje.* 1994. 10-1/2in (26cm); blonde mohair; glass eyes; fully jointed; poly-pellet stuffing; cotton checkered dress; hand-knitted woolen cardigan. Limited edition of 10. (Right) *Lars.* 1994. 12in (30cm); light cinnamon colored mohair; glass eyes; fully jointed; poly-pellet stuffing; Manchester (corduroy) trousers; tweed jumper. Limited edition of 10. (Front) *Mitch.* 1994. 4-1/2in (11cm); pale blonde mohair; glass eyes; fully jointed; kapok filled. Limited edition of 15. *Photograph by Ad Roos.*

Annemieke Koetse
BOEFJE BEARS

223. Annemieke Koetse believes in keeping a notebook beside her bed, as some of her best inspirations for her world-renowned Teddy Bears have come to her while she is relaxed.

When I was not quite a year old, I got "Bear," who turned out to be a childhood companion of great importance. He was my friend and I knitted his first breeches when I was hardly four years old. Later I made more handmade clothes. From that time, material became a way to express myself and the leading thread running through my life.

I chose to attend the Haute Couture School in Amsterdam and followed that with a few years of sculpture lessons. After my first child was born, I opened a baby/children's wear shop called "Boefje," which means a little naughty, mischievous child. After 11 years, the shop was sold. But "Bear" pursued me and I taught myself bear making.

I won the first People's choice prize at an International Festival in May 1994 and then the First Prize at the Amerongen festival in 1994, among others. The bear which won the Amerongen competition came about by throwing every conventional concept overboard. The theme was "Memories" and I incorporated a book, a strangely bent arm and mohair for an "old look." He turned out to be too small to sit on the book, so I cut the pages of the book and he ended up in the book instead. I felt very guilty cutting up those antiquated books and made a very limited edition of five "Bear in Book."

I give workshops organized by Congres-Center the "Leeuwenhorst" in Noordwijkerhout. They last one full week-end and my pupils learn how to make a bear. I also teach them how to design and create their own bears.

BEAR MAKING HINTS:
1. Keep a notebook beside your bed. You can write and/or draw all those inspiring thoughts you get when you are relaxed.
2. Don't start a business with a friend. The temperament and creativity are never on the same level and after a short time your friendship will suffer.

3. To make footpads easier to balance in the center, I create a notch at the top and bottom. (Do not shape the points into the foot pattern).
4. In making a chin and to ensure a symmetrical nose, sew the chin line halfway; pin the middle of the gusset to this middle of the line and sew it firmly; then finish the chin line.

224. *Jutter.* 1995. 11in (28cm); off-white sparse mohair; black glass eyes; fully jointed; stockinet bathing suit; paper hat; necklace of shells; toy boat. Limited edition of 25. *Jutter* (meaning beachcomber) was pictured on the cover of the spring edition of the Dutch magazine *Beerbericht.*

225. *Bibber.* 1995. 11in (28cm); gold crushed wool velvet; glass eyes; fully jointed; dress made from an original Dutch handkerchief; miniature wooden clogs. Limited edition of 10. Made exclusively for Japan Teddy Bear Association's 1995 convention in Tokyo.

Diana Olsder
DIANA'S BEREN

I think the best advice I can offer any new bear maker is to train yourself to make good Teddy Bears, before you go out to market them. For example, I made my first bear in 1986 and didn't begin re-selling them until four years later.

Most of my bears are one-of-a-kind limited editions of three to five bears. I create about 80 bears a year of all sizes. Most of them are realistic in nature.

My favorite story of the unusual bear making opportunity is when I was requested to make a copy of an old Teddy Bear for a child who had lost his original bear. All he had was a photo to go on. The end result made him very happy.

226 Bert and Diana Olsder exhibited their work at the Amerongon 1994 bear event in Holland.

227. *Stare Nose.* 1995. 13-3/4in (35cm); pale blonde mohair; plastic safety eyes; fully jointed body. Representing the first bear on Mars. All accessories are made by Bert Olsder. One-of-a-kind.

111

Yvonne Plakké
YVONNE PLAKKÉ ORIGINALS

My whole life has been under the spell of bears. As long as I remember I have had a "thing" with bears. As a child I played with bears and miniature cars, never with dolls, like other little girls.

My own bear making story started about 12 years ago. I had a very busy job as a secretary and went to school in the evenings. To relax I made handicrafts. I think this was to compensate for all the thinking during those frantic days. I made my first bear, which wasn't a real "Teddy Bear" but a little cuddly toy made of terry cloth for my friend's first baby.

I make bears for people who are cramped for space. I lived in a very small apartment for many years. There wasn't any room for bears. So I just made small ones, so they could sit all cozy next to each other without taking up too much space.

I aim to make bears with a certain nostalgic magic, which is the reason I will never make them with strange heads or limbs. I think this is very ingenious for other bear artists perhaps, but not for me.

I make my bears completely by myself. I do have a friend who does the knitting for me after I show her the pattern. But, I am the one who chooses the materials for the sweaters. Another friend makes the old fashioned dresses for me, again, according to my pattern. This is the only way for me to work, creating my own bears. I find other people's work is always different from your own.

I produce around 400 (5—12in {13—31cm}) bears a year and market them at approximately ten shows (two or three in England, two in Japan, two in Germany, and three or four in Holland).

228. "My whole life has been under the spell of bears. As long as I can remember I have had a fascination and love of Teddy Bears," says Yvonne Plakké. Today Yvonne's goal is to create Teddy Bears with a nostalgic magic.

229. *Swimpy.* (All three bears are same design). 1995. 9-1/2in (24cm); antique gold short pile mohair; sheepswool and pellet stuffing; black glass eyes; and fully jointed. Each bear wears an old-fashioned bathing suit and comes with a sunchair.

Léon & Hedy Romans van Schaik
HUGABLE BEARS

After seeing Ted Menten's bears I had a different outlook on Teddy Bears. I wanted to make character bears, instead of traditional bears. But now, in addition to the miniature bears I make, I also make monkeys, porcupines, rabbits, dogs, and owls.

I was the first male bear-artist and the first character bear maker in Holland. Even though I make all of the bears, we are becoming a family business. Our bears' characteristics include their big underbelly, big claws, and wrinkles. They also all wear a pearl on their heart and a card with our name and trademark.

We do about eight shows and make 80 to 100 bears a year. They range from very small (3-1/2in {6cm}) to much larger (39-1/2in {95cm}). I work in both upholstery (for the smaller bears) and mohair (for the bigger ones and other animals).

We are very fortunate. Our bears seem to sell themselves; and some of them we have a hard time selling because we get so attached to them.

230. Léon Romans van Schaik has not only earned recognition for his line of "Hugable Bears," but his character animals have brought him praise and popularity among his fellow artists and collectors.

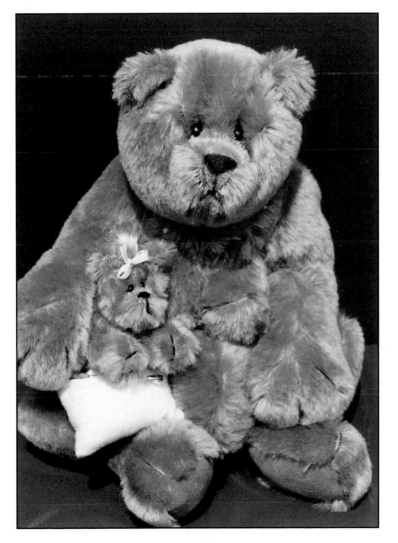

231. *Mum and Bebe.* 1995. *Mum* is 9-3/4in (25cm); (sitting); tan colored mohair; black button eyes; fully jointed. Note the big paws, expressive face and breasts on *Mum.*

Audie F. Sison
A TEDDY...BY AUDIE

A native of the Philippines, I moved to Europe in 1986 after working for seven years with the Philippine Ministry of Tourism. I lived in Spain for almost six years. There, I studied Spanish and Philosophy. I also took up drawing and painting courses. I spent a year in Greece before I finally settled in Holland.

It was here in The Netherlands where I learned everything about the Teddy Bear. In 1990, I started collecting Teddy Bears made by artists from the U.S.A., U.K., and local Dutch artists. In the summer of 1994, I began making my own.

Many American artists have inspired me along the way especially Kathy Wallace, Regina Brock, Pat Murphy, Mary George, and Frances Harper.

As I am a very new bear maker, I must say that I'm still in the process of learning many things about this art. But, I have learned not to hesitate to consult or ask advice from senior artists for problems that I encounter in making bears. It is not enough to be creative, or to have the technical know-how in bear making. You must have a lot of patience and determination to make bears. Sometimes just one teddy requires several painstaking hours—or even days—to make!

My style is classic/traditional Teddy Bears and I make about 100-150 a year. Mostly they are one-of-a-kind, but some are limited editions. They all have a sewn-in label at the back of the right thigh. I sell them for $150-$550 and they range from 12—32in (31—81cm).

I have lots of plans for the future. I would like to participate in more International Bears Shows, in Europe and also America, Australia, and Japan. As I grow, I hope to be able to perfect my workmanship and would very much like to learn and know everything about bear making and then...to be able to share this knowledge with future bear makers.

BEAR MAKING HINTS:
1. Read various types of books or manuals on bear making. This will help develop your creativity in making and designing your own concept of a Teddy Bear.
2. Learn how several artists/bearmakers make their own pattern and how they create their bears.
3. Be daring and experiment further by using different types and color of mohair and changing the direction of the pile. Vary the expression of the face by using other sizes and colors or position of the eyes, ears, nose and mouth. Use or combine various kinds of stuffing materials to give your bear that special feel.

232. A native of the Philippines, Audie Sison finally made Holland his home. It was here he discovered his love and talent for creating his outstanding nostalgic looking bears.

233. *Casimir.* 1995. 24in (61cm); antique blonde feather finish English mohair; glass eyes; fully jointed; wonderful long curved arms; wears a blue knitted jumper.

Riet Slump
BUZZY BEAR

I come from a creative family; I learned to make wooden figures from my granddad and how to make children's clothing and patterns from my mother. Before I made bears, I was a hairdresser and painted. I once made a lovely oil-painting of my husband's old Teddy Bear, together with a new bear which I made for my daughter. Once I really started making bears, I stopped painting.

Most of my bears are children and range from 14—15-1/2in (10—40cm) high.

I am finding it increasingly difficult to stuff the bears. Since my bears are firmly stuffed and quite heavy, I can hardly use my hands because of the intensity of the work. I have been making 60 to 80
Continued on page 115.

234. Riet Slump's adorable bears are not only popular among Dutch collectors but they have been on Mirja De Vries' beautiful postcards.

bears a year, but perhaps I will make fewer, but even more beautiful ones in the years to come.

I am proud to be among a group of 15 of my fellow top bear artists in Holland who started a group called "Excellent Bearmakers." I was also honored to win the logo contest in 1992; the task was to make the emblem of the club in three dimensions and my attempt was selected as the best.

A final note, once a bear is ready, I cut the hair from the inner-ear, so teddy can listen to everything you want to tell him.

BEAR MAKING HINTS:
1. To help the bears stand on their own, use a very fine grain in their feet to make them heavy.
2. Sew the whole head of the bear and cut it open at the back. This way the stuffing can be more precise.

Jonette Stabbert
POPPETTE DOLL STUDIO

235. Jonette Stabbert has worked in many different areas of the art world. She works in many different mediums and is able to think "three-dimensionally." This is a tremendous advantage to her. This magnificent array of bears Jonette produced from 1992 to 1995 is an example of the variety this artist includes in her line of Poppette Bears.

I am considered the first professional Teddy Bear artist in the Netherlands. Because of my reputation, I was invited to the Teddy Bear convention at Disney World®, Florida in 1993 to represent "bear artistry" for all of continental Europe. It is important to mention that my friend and colleague, Edith Luitink has been making realistic bears since the seventies. Of course, she too is a fantastic bear artist, and now also makes teddies sometimes.

I have a very extensive art background and was considered a child "prodigy," taking sculpting and painting lessons with well-known artist through special programs at the Brooklyn Museum of Art. I attended Washington Irving High School's special art division and studied briefly at the Fashion Institute of Technology in New York. I learned to work in a huge range of materials while working in the theater and this helped me to design special props for ad agencies and has been the most important training for creating my bears and other toys. It is a tremendous advantage to work in different media and to think "three-dimensionally."

I don't confine myself to one particular style. My bears range from itsy-bitsy to "humongous," from fantasy to traditional to realistic. I don't like frowning bears. Only my bears with teeth look ferocious, the rest have sweet or wistful faces. The "Toothy Teds" are probably the most creatively challenging of my designs, and give me the most artistic satisfaction. I hand sculpt every tooth individually.

I have a huge dog who looks a lot like a bear. I use his teeth and nose as models for my work. Sometimes he hides if I look inside his mouth too much. This work has been difficult and time consuming. I make raised gums from velour, then implant every molar and canine separately, then insert the tongue. I also hand sculpt the claws and have several methods for making raised paw cushions. I often hand-color the eyes, and love working with thermo-plastics and resins to make eyes and teeth and for other little special touches. Some of my miniature bears are also realistic and I like to make tableaus of natural settings in which I place them.

I very seldom do shows, but sell to individual collectors and to shops. I have two sales reps in the U.S., but handle my own sales everywhere else.

I have a lot of "secret" customers. There are men who are closet arctophiles, but dare not let anyone know. They actually carry my miniature bears hidden in a pocket as a companion. I find it very touching when an outwardly cold, very businesslike man, conservatively dressed, suddenly gets this soft expression and talks tenderly to his little bear!

Dimph van Gemert
SKINLE BEAR

236. Dimph van Gemert's bears represent traditional and realistic looking designs.

Even though I have received some incredible awards and recognition, I want my bear making to remain a hobby, not a business. The big bear show in Amerongen inspired me immensely. I started selling bears the very same year I saw the possibilities at that show (1991). I took eight bears to a small show and they sold out in one morning!

In 1992, I was given a special prize by John Blackburn of Canterbury Bears in England. The next year I won the first prize in the European Teddy Bear contest at Amerongen. I was just as thrilled with the gift Mr. Blackburn sent me the very same day our youngest son Sander, was born. It was a bear called *Long John* and he was the very same size as the baby. What a fond memory!

Demand is forcing me to make more bears than I used to. I get many orders and probably make 30-40 bears a year. They are all mohair, with glass eyes and leather footpads and noses. I make two kinds of bears: authentic Teddy Bears with sweet faces and detailed accessories such as collars and hats; and naturalistic bears with genuine footpads and noses. On the natural type bears, the footpads are fully detailed as are the contours of the body. They even have wet tongues and eyes. My smallest undressed bear sells for $75; the most expensive is about $300.

I have both limited and open editions. The limited editions come with a special certificate, which is signed and numbered. All my bears wear a special cloth-tag which is sewed in the back seam. It reads: Skinle Bear, Dimph van Gemert, Schijndel.

237. A representation of the quality of work of Dimph's traditional bears. (Back row, left to right). *Isodorus.* 8in (22cm); *Casper.* 10in (26cm); *Frederick.* 10in (26cm); (Front row left to right). *L'automne.* 10in (26cm); *Ferdinand.* 4in (11cm); *Eduard.* 9in (23cm); *Fleur.* 9in (23cm).

116

Vera van Oeveren
O'FAMILY COLLECTIBLES

It is difficult to establish a good name in the bear making world. To be recognized you have to invest a lot of time and hard work. When you finally get a name, you have to work even harder to keep the name honorable. Competition is fierce but that's what makes for more interesting and unique bear creations.

I am fortunate in that I had a great name to work with from the very start, my mother Francis Osephius. I "apprenticed" by helping her at Doll and Bear Exhibitions in Holland when she was "Francy Bears." When I started making my own bears, I took some to an exhibition and there I sold my first one. It went so well we decided to go together under one name. We make the bears separately, using our own designs and mohair.

238. Vera van Oeveren has her arms full with two of her great looking 1995 bruins. Pictured on the left is *Oliver* and on the right is *George*. *Photograph by Fotoburo Henk van Veen.*

All of my bears are handmade by me, from the beginning till the end. My mother makes their clothes. I choose the fabric and tell her how I want the clothes to be and my dad also helps. He makes the joints and when we need something special, like a wooden wheelbarrow for the country bears, he does that too. I can't forget my husband, Ron, as he gives us a lot of support and always gives an honest opinion about the bears I make. (He likes almost all of them!)

My bear making is a little bit like the "American style." Many American artists put a lot of fantasy in their bears and I try to do that as well. I like to make bears based on certain figures. For example, *Dik Trom*, a bear on a donkey, is based on a famous Dutch book figure. (He was selected for the "Publieksprijs 1994" at the Bearfestival at castle Amerongen).

My bears are easy to identify by their angular embroidered noses and funny long ears. Their bodies are relatively long and filled with fiberfill, pellets, or a combination of pellets and fiberfill. When I use pellets, I fill them softly. If not, they are filled pretty strong. They always have glass eyes (mostly black). I use natural colors of mohair, alpaca, or a combination of mohair/alpaca or silk/alpaca for their coats. Except for my one-of-a-kind Jester bears which have colored mohair.

My bears range in price from 6in (15cm) at $110 all the way to 20-1/2—25in (55—60cm) at $390.

Before they are sold, all the bears I make get a place in my living room so I can see them and enjoy them for the time they are mine. That gives me so much pleasure.

239. (Left) *Tilly* and rabbit *Floortje*. 1995. 15-1/2in (40cm); golden colored German mohair; glass black eyes; fully jointed. One-of-a-kind. (Center front) *Henry and William*. 1995. 10-1/2in (24cm); golden colored German mohair; glass eyes; fully jointed. Limited edition of 2. (Right) *Harold*. 1995. 16-3/4in (40cm); golden colored German mohair; glass black eyes; fully jointed. Comes with wooden wheelbarrow filled with vegetables and chickens. One-of-a-kind. *Photograph by Fotoburo Henk van Veen.*

117

Chapter 10

FRENCH TEDDY BEAR ARTISTS

Aline Cousin
MY BEAR TO ME

240. Aline Cousin exhibits her handmade bear creations at the Toymania Show held in Paris, France. Peeking into the bottom of the picture are some of Aline's old French teddies.

I think I am the first one to make artist bears in France! I began in 1990, when I saw, a little white Steiff bear. I tried to make another one with cotton and old plush. In 1991, I made my first Teddy Bear with mohair I ordered from the U.K.

I make my own patterns and prefer the old fashioned Teddy Bears. I really enjoy the sewing of the bears, but the stuffing is difficult for me. I produce about 50 bears a year and also repair old Teddy Bears.

My bears range from 4—20in (10—51cm); I sell them for $100 to $250. I go to about four shows during the year.

Since 1992 I have run the French Teddy Bear Club (Club Françáis de L'Ours Ancien).

241. (Left) *Berlingot*. 1994. 19-1/2in (50cm); honey colored mohair; old black shoe-button eyes; fully jointed. Limited edition of 25. (Center) *Pierrot*. 1994. 4in (10cm); white mohair; glass eyes; fully jointed. One-of-a-kind. (Right) *Muzo*. 1992. 10in (25cm); short light beige mohair; black shoe-button eyes; fully jointed. Limited edition of 25.

Marylou Jouet
JOUETEDDY

(My appreciation to Sherry Champeaux who helped me communicate my thoughts to you in English).

In France, nothing exists for bear making. We are very behind your country, and because of this, plus the problem of non-existent supplies, very few people have made bears.

It is quite coincidental that my name is "Jouet" since that translates into "toy" in English. I write in white ink on my labels "Made with love-Keep me forever" and I sign it "Mme JOUET", so that everyone can understand my name. My label is also an adoption certificate and on the right side the limited edition number with the bear's name and composition is written.

My bears are made entirely in the traditional way, with wood wool stuffing and with hardboard fully jointed limbs. I use only glass eyes and real antique boot buttons for my special patchwork bears.

Presently I make about 100 bears a year of all sizes. My husband helps me joint the big bears because we only use cotter-pin joints and hardboard disks.

Because there are not very many bear artists in France, a friend of mine and I formed a club for all friends of Teddy Bears called Le Club des Amis de L'ours." (The Teddy's Patch).

242. Marylou Jouet's love of Teddy Bears led her to create her own distinct line.

243. *Crocsou* (Coin purse bear). 1995. 6-5/8in (17cm); short honey colored German mohair; glass eyes; fully jointed. Old beads decorate metal top of purse.

Ulrike Amadori
DIE WERKSTATT

I had been making collectible dolls, but my then, seven year old, son Peter, did not like dolls. So, I made him a Teddy Bear. So, since 1992, I have made classic bears, funny bears, and natural bears. In 1994, I won first place in the "award-of-the-public" at Aachen/Germany, Euro teddy show.

I work alone, but if he has time, my husband helps me. I make approximately 150 mohair bears a year, mostly one-of-a-kind or limited editions up to five. I sell most of them myself but also a few bear shops carry them. The small 6in (15cm) sells for DM 130 (approximately $89). The larger 28in (71cm) goes for DM 700 (approximately $482).

I am just learning about the business aspect of bear making. I have realized there is a great difference between Germany and America, or England. Here it is not easy to sell unusual bears or original bears. Then, you go to a show and the very next show you see your bears, your noses, your dresses, over and over.

Perhaps the most satisfying part of making bears for me is creating new patterns for teddies and making my bears as natural as possible.

244. Ulrike Amadori works alone, and produces approximately 150 mohair bears a year.

245. Ulrike Amadori's son Peter shares his mother's fascination with Teddy Bears. Ulrike's big bruin *Dimitrij* affectionately has his arm around Peter as they both endearingly look at Ulrike's little bear *Jossi*.

246. (Top to bottom) *Old Henry* 20-1/2in (52cm), *Jonny* 11-3/4in (30cm), *Hans* 13-1/2in (34cm) and *Jossi* 6in (15cm). All bears are crafted of different colors of mohair, have fully jointed bodies and glass eyes. Produced in 1995 in limited editions of up to 5.

Marie Robischon
ROBIN DER BÄR, CREATION MARIE

Even as a little girl I made small bears for my dollhouse which my father had built for me. For these tiny bears, I used small patches of material. Though they were not perfect I loved them and they were great to play with. Later I created Teddy Bears and other stuffed animals for my children. Then, in the late eighties, I sold the first samples which were more professional.

I have made stuffed animals of all kinds and of the most different materials for my sons. Now I create bears in the classic style and materials which were always used in manufacturing teddies: mohair, wooden wool, glass eyes, or antique shoe-button eyes. These traditional bears have serious faces, long arms, and *Continued on page 121.*

247. Marie Robischon works alone when creating her magnificent bears. Marie feels it is impossible for her to instruct someone to work on the countless different details her bear creations require.

248. Leather bears. 1994—1995. Smooth and rough leather is used to create these unique looking bears and their fine looking outfits.

Marie Robischon
ROBIN DER BÄR, CREATION MARIE

large feet. They are dressed in solid clothes which are so durable that they can be worn for life. The clothes are often enhanced with antique accessories and often made from antique materials. They take a long time to make because of their detailed apparel. I also make bears from old military woolen cloth, rough linen, or leather.

My bears are sold to antique and new toy specialty stores in Basel, Berlin, and London. Most of the time I do not like bear fairs because they are so commercial. However, I did enjoy the big London Bear Fair in Kensington in 1995. I plan to attend others in the future, such as the big German Bear Fair held in April each year.

249. *Oldie.* 1995. 17in (44cm); dark gold curly mohair; black glass eyes; fully jointed; wood shavings and wool stuffing (stuffed softer for antique look). Dressed in black helmet with lion ornament, old bright red wool jacket with old buttons, and appliqué lined with red silk. Trousers are black wool.

250. *Pirate.* 1995. 17-1/4in (44cm); long dark gold curly mohair; black glass eyes; fully jointed; stuffed with wood shavings and wool. Suit is made in 19th century fashion, long jacket, red brown velvet with mauve appliqué on arms, old buttons, leather belt with toy gun. Trousers are made of old linen with leather appliqué, necklace of coins.

121

251. Dagmar Strunck surrounded by a representation of her bear creations.

252. *Uliz the Colorful Bear* (left) with his brother (right). 1995. 31-1/2in (80cm). For Dagmar, *Uliz* is a physical manifestation of her visions and her standpoint in philosophy. The vibrant colors and artistic designs are hand painted by Dagmar onto the mohair before it is cut.

Dagmar Strunck
BÄRENHÖHLE DER TEDDYLADEN

I made my first bear because I was angry with the German post for losing a parcel of bears from Whatabear in California. We had ordered them for our Teddy Bear shop. I was so angry that I took a piece of paper, painted a pattern, took a piece of plush, and made my first bear, *Rudolph*. It turned out he was the winner of the *Hugglets* competition in the summer of 1993 at the Kensington fair as the Best Dressed Bear.

All my bears are jointed and they are somewhere between human beings and natural bears. In addition to the award that *Rudolph* won, *Willi* bear was selected by three Doll and Toy Museums in Neustadt, Coburg, and Sonneberg as the Best Artist Bear in Germany in 1994. A display of five bears, entitled "Justice," won second place in the European Championship in 1994.

I always wanted to be an artist, but had to learn a commercial job. However, I started collecting bears in 1990 and two years later we rented a small shop for English collector bears. We started with 42 different teddies, now we have 150 to 200 artist bears at a time, adding a hundred or so new ones every other month.

I sell my bears retail in my shop in Germany and at fairs in Germany, America, and Great Britain. I also sell my bears wholesale in those countries and through the Museum Shop in Naples, Florida.

My first year I made 150 bears. The second I produced more than 350 and now I am producing about 400 bears per year. They are priced at $120 for a 10in (25cm) up to $300 for a 23in (58cm).

I feel that I am in good company with many artists when it comes to bearmaking. From the beginning of human life to today, people have been very close to bears. I respect the free life of every form on earth. In my work, I try to show that the earth is full of wonder and I invite all people to follow me in my world.

I am grateful to my grandpa Heinrich and my father-in-law who have both shown me to work with my hands, to see with my eyes, keep the dream in front of me, and to keep a cool head in critical times.

253. Dagmar and Bernd Strunck's attractive booth at a Christmas show in Germany. Dagmar has become known in the bear world for creating bears with extreme character.

122

Noriko Aoyagi

I make bears like boys. But, my background began with making replicas of European dresses of the Middle Ages. I also made original dresses (I graduated with a degree in dress and ornaments).

At any rate, today I make approximately 100-130 bears a year and they range from 1—17in (3—45cm). They range in price from approximately $50 to $220. Mainly I sell wholesale, but do retail at two Teddy Bear fairs a year.

I do teach a hand-made Teddy Bear class in Tokyo. I tell my students to be happy when making bears, because your feelings are reflected in the faces of the bears.

254. Japanese artists are known for their interest and talent in creating miniature items of great detail. Therefore, it is a natural tendency for many Japanese artists to create miniature Teddy Bears. Noriko Aoyagi is one of Japan's well-known miniature artists.

Etsuko Hasegawa
STAR CHILD CO., LTD.

My father, Ekyu Hasegawa, established the Hasegawa Toy Company as a workshop for the export business of soft toy assembly in 1952. Five years after its inception the company sold 30,000 Teddy Bears to the U.S. market. By 1960 we were making stuffed animals with swivel necks and music boxes for the U.S. and European market. By 1970 we sold 50,000 units a year and soon afterwards started to export the stuffed animal with soft touch cloth. Today, the Hasegawa Toy Company and Star Child Co., Ltd. sell their products to the domestic market with wide variations of soft toys and sport accessories. Additionally, we will make further efforts to create beloved Teddy Bears for customers all over the world.

I work as a designer for my father's firm and both he and my elder brother have influenced me greatly. I began making stuffed animals of all sorts in the second grade as a hobby and exhibited hand-made bears professionally for the first time in 1995.

In Japan, unfortunately, we do not have a tradition of Teddy Bears. We do not give them as baby shower gifts. Many children do not grow up with bears. However, we at Star Child, are working toward establishing some kind of traditional Teddy Bear culture in Japan. Our goal is to continue to design our original products keeping in mind the peace, love, and dreams they will give all our customers.

255. Etsuko Hasegawa (right) inherits her artistic talents and her love of Teddy Bears from her father, Ekyu Hasegawa (left), founder and owner of the soft toy company Star Child. Ekyu Hasegawa proudly holds an example of one of his beautiful 1957 100% Rayon designs from the Hasegawa Toy Company

256. *Fight! Kobe.* 1995. 14in (36cm). Blonde colored acrylic body; 100% Rayon outfit (an integral part of body); plastic eyes; fully jointed; self standing. Etsuko created this bear as an expression of her feelings for the Kobe earthquake victims.

Manami Horii

I was just thirteen years old when I made a bear for the first time. I was sitting in math class and the geometric figures suggested a pattern of a Teddy Bear.

I sincerely like the antique and traditional looking bears. I make about 30 a year now and prices are from $50 to $500.

The international quality of bear making is especially dear to me. Through bears, people find me interesting. I truly enjoy making friends all over the world. I hope I'll have the opportunity to live in many countries and have a shop some day.

257. Teddy Bear making has become extremely popular in Japan among the younger generation. Manami Horii's production is quite limited therefore she enjoys making one-of-a-kind bears.

Reiko Hoshino

After seeing bears made by Linda Spiegel-Lohre I was inspired to try it myself. Since then I have been making approximately 70 one-of-a-kind miniature bears a year. They have big noses, small eyes, and look like naughty but nice little boys.

Making bears has broadened my life and made it much happier. If I had one piece of advice to beginners trying their hand at bear making it would be to approach it like making dinner for your sweetheart — with lots of love!

258. Reiko Hoshino's favorite bear design, her chubby cheeked bear (left and center), always bring a smile to collectors' faces.

259. Reiko Hoshino uses various types of fabrics and colors when she creates her whimsical miniature bears and animals.

124

Kazuko Ichikawa

I was a toy designer in a big company. My work was interesting, but I wanted to make something by hand, not for mass production. The first bear I made was not too good. But I was happy. Teddy Bears made me happy and I wanted to make more.

I make about 100 bears a year and teach two workshops, run by NIHON VOGU SYA, my publishing company. I have made bears for a number of books on Teddy Bear making. I have also created bears for picture books on handmade bears.

I have many dreams for the future. I am always interested in making bears for books. I would also like to make a CD-ROM.

260. Kazuko Ichikawa incorporates her adorable bear creations in appealing scenes she creates for her popular Teddy Bear picture books she writes for children and collectors. *Photograph by Wataru Shiokawa.*

261. These charming little bears, are characters in Kazuko's Teddy Bear picture books. Ranging in size from 5—10in (13—25cm) their names are (top left to right) *Angie, Topy, Papu,* and (bottom) *Marshmellow.* Made of different types of mohair, each bear is fully jointed with glass eyes. *Photograph by Shinsuke Suzuki and Wataru Shiokawa.*

262. This tiny one-of-a-kind bear (4in [10cm]) was made by Kazuko Ichikawa during her plane trip on one of her many visits to America. Kazuko wrote the following caption for this enchanting picture "I never mind height difference, because I love you." *Photograph by Sinsuke Suzuki.*

Atsuko Isaji
BEARY TALES

I love bear making, but it is my last priority. First, I am the mother of my children; secondly I write reviews of mysteries and novels for girls, and lastly, I am a bear artist. Thus, I only make five to ten bears a year.

I started bearmaking at the encouragement of my husband who knew how much I loved making dolls and how much I love bears. The few bears I have sold range from $50 to $200. They are all made of mohair and have glass-eyes, so the price difference is based on size.

Sometimes at tea time I teach bearmaking to my friends. It is a very happy time.

263. Atsuko Isaji (center), a member of GBW (Good Bears of the World), translates GBW publication *Bear Tracks* into Japanese for the club members. Her love of Teddy Bears inspired her to create her own bear designs (center left) *Strawberry*, (right) *Cinnamon*. Also pictured are two of Atsuko's biggest fans, her daughter Asayo and son Youske.

Hisa Kato

264. Hisa Kato is a relatively new Teddy Bear artist who attracted lots of attention with her unique bear designs at the Japan Teddy Bear Association's 1995 convention in Tokyo.

Although I began making bears nearly a decade ago, it wasn't until last year that I sold my first bear. My love for art (I graduated from an art school with a major in oil painting) is only one of my major influences or inspirations. I get input from everything I see, hear, smell, taste, and feel.

I make the kind of bears that I like and how many I like. This translates to about 240 bears a year, predominantly one-of-a-kind. I sell them from ¥1500 to ¥100,000 (approximately $15 to $1000). They range in size from 13—60-1/2in (5—160cm). I use all kinds of fabrics.

I was very pleased to receive an award at the Third Japan Teddy Bear Convention, the first time I attended the event! I think I won because my bear looks as if it has rich emotions deep inside. Its eyes, ears, nose, and mouth may be out of position, but for such expressions to work, creators need to abandon the common sense of loveliness.

This is just the beginning. My goal is to have my very own gallery for my bears and my art works.

265. Bears made by Hisa Kato are affectionately posed around a doll also made by this creative young artist. Hisa's bears are recognized by their sweet, little wooden noses.

126

Emi Koyanagi
NEEDLE MAMA

I began making bears eight years ago but I do not really sell them. At that time, in Japan, the handmade Teddy Bears were not so popular, except among very few teddy lovers. Prior to this, I was a quilting (patchwork) teacher. I produce approximately 200 bears a year and appear at about 100 shows. Most of these shows are not to sell bears, but to promote my book.

I teach many workshops, both at a cultural center and at my home. My first book was on making Tiny Bears. I am currently writing another book on making regular sized Teddy Bears.

My bears are predominantly decent and handsome looking. It is difficult for me to make the pattern, but the greatest pleasure for me is making the dress and sewing it!

266. Emi Koyanagi teaches Teddy Bear making workshops for up to 130-150 people. She is currently writing a book on Teddy Bears.

267. *Two Faced Bears.* 1994. (Left and right) 2in (6cm); (center) 9in (23cm); gold distressed mohair bodies; short black mohair ears; fully jointed; (center) glass eyes; (left and right) one face has plastic eyes, other face has onyx bead eyes.

268. Akemi Myoujin makes her petite works of art under the name of Tinkly Little. *Photograph by Haruyo Yamaji.*

I met so many lovely bears at Mr. Onozuka's Teddy Bear shop called "Cuddly Brown" in Tokyo. That made me eager to make bears myself. In fact, one of my goals is to become the artist who makes the "Cuddly Brown" anniversary bear because that shop is so special for me.

I also yearn to make bears as small and as exquisite as I can. I mainly make miniature bears with antique parts. They are quite small ranging from 1—3in (3—8cm). Some people think my price range is high ($60-$90) because my bears are so small. However, I only make 60 bears a year that are very exact.

I teach a class held by "Cuddly Brown" and also a class at Japan Vogue. You can also find my bears at the Teddy Bear Museum in Kobe, as well as photographs and patterns of my bears which appeared on two books published by Japan Vogue Co., (1994 and 1995) and two other books published by Ondori-Sha Co., Ltd. in those same years.

Hikari Ohnishi
HIKARI OHNISHI DESIGN ROOM

I have worked for 28 years as a free-lance designer in the field of crafts using cloth, especially patchwork, knitting, embroidery, dresses, corsages, and stuffed animals and dolls. I have my own workshops and classes for patchwork and other handicrafts.

It was the publisher of my book, Patchwork Zoo, who asked me to include some bears in the book. This was in 1984. Now I only present bears in publications and occasionally sell them by request. When I have an order, I make a bear in accordance with the client's preference of color and sell it with two sets of outfits.

I have participated in the Tokyo Bear Show three times, and during the past three years I have made some 100 bears. If I have an order I can make a 16in (41cm) bear in a day. I sell them for ¥15,000 to ¥20,000 (approximately $150 to $200), excluding mailing charge.

BEAR MAKING HINTS:
1. To get a better finish, sew with finer stitching and make some notches in the seam allowance at a curve perpendicular to it.
2. To prevent the decrease in volume of synthetic cotton, fill the body rigidly with small tweezers, little by little.
3. Choose dress colors suitable to the color of your bear.
4. You can collect the fine dust of the fur if you cover your knees with a nylon scarf during bear making.

269. Hikari Ohnishi is seated in the park with two of her cuddly bears she named after my husband (left) Wally and me (right) Linda.

270. (Left to right) *Chuchu,* 9in (23cm); *Mamy,* 15in (38cm); *Poemun,* 11-3/4in (30cm). All bears are made of acrylic plush; fully jointed with plastic eyes. Clothes are handmade by the artist. Each bear is sold with two outfits.

129

Miki Saito
KALI BEARS

I feel there is a special expressionless, almost sorrowful beauty particular to the Japanese checkered dolls. I have tried to emulate this in my bears.

When my two year old daughter was born, I couldn't find my favorite style stuffed bears, so I thought I would give it a try and make one. She was not interested in bears filled with wood wool of a smaller size. She was always holding a soft type in her arms. However, when making a bear of some larger size (23-1/2in {60cm}) and filled with wood wool, she liked it a lot. She embraced it, wrestled with it, danced with it and watched TV with it. It seemed that a life-sized bear has a special role as a companion or friend for a small child.

I work entirely by myself and have been honored with a couple of prizes at the Japan Teddy Bear Convention. I make about 100 bears annually and attend three shows. I also sell at six retail outlets in Tokyo. I am looking forward to the time when Teddy Bear making can become my main source of income.

271. Miki Saito is one of the few artists in Japan that produce a vintage style bear.

272. (Left to right) *Parade.* 1995. 15-3/4in (40cm); cinnamon colored mohair; glass eyes; fully jointed. *Pablo.* 1995. 23-3/4in (60cm); brown wavy mohair; glass eyes; fully jointed. P.P. 150. 1995. 13in (35cm); light blonde mohair; shoe button eyes; fully jointed. P.P. 150's design was inspired by Steiff's early elephant button bears. *Photograph by Masato Tashir.*

130

Hiroyuki Sakata
GACHA GACHA

It is very rewarding for me to create something with my own hands. On top of that, to have people admire and appreciate them gives me so much pleasure.

I only make about 50 bears a year. It is frustrating to not be able to make larger quantities, but they are mostly all hand made and it is very time-consuming and impossible to make in larger numbers. Luckily my bears have been very well received, and they appear to give their new owners much happiness. But, still, I would be very pleased if I could make even more people happy in the same way.

Due to high prices for supplies in Japan, it is not possible to make bears of substantial size reasonably. By the time my bears are completed, a lot of money, as well as time, has gone into their production and therefore, prices can be quite high. This has made Japanese collectors and interested buyers very selective. And, unfortunately, some potential buyers just cannot afford to make the purchases.

We price bears, they range from ¥10,000 to ¥70,000 (approximately $100 to $700). The less expensive bears are approximately 4in (10cm) tall and the larger bears are about 23-1/2in (60cm) tall.

I teach a regular bear making class weekly and have even taught an all men's bear making class! My bears have been written up in Japanese publications, such as *My Teddy Bear*, Volume 4, and *Teddy Bear Voice*.

My bears may be just your standard bears...but they have pure hearts and souls. Someday I hope my bears will be seen and appreciated by people from all over the world.

273. Hiroyuki Sakata is proud to have had his bears written up in Japanese publications, such as *My Teddy Bear* (Volume 4), and *Teddy Bear Voice.* He teaches a regular bear making class weekly and has even taught an all men's bear making class.

274. *Bears.* 1994. 13-1/2in (35cm). Various colors of high quality straight mohair are used to produce these magnificently regal looking bruins. Each bear is fully jointed with elongated characteristics and glass eyes.

131

275. Tomoko Suenaga works intensely to maintain the perfection and originality standards she sets for herself when making each of her charming bears.

Someday, in the future, I hope that we have a voluntary group like Good Bears of the World in Japan. I know that the warmth of a bear gives handicapped children power. My mother and I began sending bears to handicapped children in 1994. Just knowing that my bears make people smile is truly a reward. In fact, one of my lines is called Kindness Bears. I produce more of those that are the same than any other.

It was *Cuddly Bear* by Linda Spiegel-Lohre who inspired me to make bears and the photos of the Romerhaus Bears that brought me into making miniature bears. But it was truly my mother who taught me the skills to make bears.

This year I won first and second place at the Japan Teddy Bear Association convention. Also, my bear "Lucky" was selected to be the featured miniature bear in the May/June (1995) issue of *Teddy Bear and Friends®* magazine.

I only exhibit once a year and produce 60 to 70 bears. I make each bear by hand so that each has his own loving expression and personality.

The standard price is about $80 for a 2-1/2in (6cm) bear with synthetic fabric, five joints, and onyx or glass eyes.

The most pleasure in making my bears is when the bear is finished and it looks at me as if he were saying, "Hello! Thanks for giving me a life!"

276. *Lapine.* 1995. 3in (8cm); pale beige synthetic fabric, black onyx bead eyes; fully jointed. One-of-a-kind. Applying eyelids and bunny ears expresses the bear's wish to be a rabbit.

277. *Jo.* 1994. 2in (5cm); pale cream colored synthetic fabric; glass bead eyes; fully jointed. One-of-a-kind.

Masami Sugahara
MY OWN TEDDY

278. Masami Sugahara smiles as she proudly gives her bear creations an approving look.

I had been studying 3-D animation at the School of the Art Institute of Chicago for several years. It was there that I first saw a Teddy Bear magazine. I was so excited to discover the numerous ways people expressed themselves through bears.

As I explored clay sculpting, drawing, museum illustration, and focused on creating various kinds of characters in puppet animation, the experiences helped me to create a basis for creating interesting and fascinating bears.

It was in the summer of 1993 that I began making bears for sale. I try to create bears that people want to take home. My emphasis is on bears which look like they could live on their own. This comes from my background in puppet animation.

My mother works with me. She knits bear costumes and helps me at the one or two shows I do a year. I produce about a 100 bears a year. Each is an individual and they range in size from very tiny, 1-1/2in (4cm) to much larger, 30-1/2in (78cm). They are priced from $45 to $500.

This pricing is the hardest task and I always tell myself, "the bears have to be what the bear lovers really want."

In the future, I plan to create many more characters besides bears. I would really like to shoot puppet animation films and include my creations.

279. (Left) *Densuke.* 1994. 10in (25cm); pink rayon; ultrasuede paw pads; German glass googlie eyes; fully jointed; open mouth. Wire frame creates posable arms and legs. Wearing hand-knitted vest. (Right) *Noël.* 1994. 11in (28cm); green rayon; ultrasuede paw pads; German plastic eyes; fully jointed. Wireframe encased in arms and legs. One-of-a-kind. *Photograph by Masato Sugahara.*

133

280. Creating original designs does not come easy for Okiyasu Sugi, however, he combats this by looking through books, going to shows and antique shops, and looking at as many bears as possible. *Photograph by Kazunaga Kato.*

281. *Piewie.* 1994. 15-3/4in (40cm); black viscose; cream viscose inset lower face and snout; glass eyes; fully jointed; one-of-a-kind bear with immense character and appealing body characteristics. *Photograph by Kazunaga Kato.*

I haven't been making bears very long. A friend asked me to try and I've been at it ever since. I have always enjoyed art and have done some illustration work for Japanese magazines as well as drawing patterns for paper dolls. Once I worked as an assistant for a Japanese contemporary artist.

I price my bears from ¥10,000 (approximately $100) and up. I have made both large and small bears. Now I am concentrating on miniature bears (1-1/2in {4cm}).

At one of the shows here in Japan, one visitor was examining my miniature bears and asked: "Is there some sort of magic that is involved in making bears so small and exact?" That made me laugh and really stuck in my mind, because I particularly enjoy making bears that are precisely and intricately made. I also like to make slightly unusual patterns for my bears. Because of their detail, I only make about 60 a year and most of them are one-of-a-kind (but I have done some limited editions).

However, originality is not easy for me. Individuality does not come quickly and this has been frustrating. One way I combat this is to look through different books and go to shows and antique shops to look at as many bears as I can. I always keep searching for those bears that suit me the best, or that I like the best. These are helping me improve my own creations and grow as an artist.

282. (Left to right). *Big Ear, York, Honey* and *Jimmy.* 1995. Average size 1-1/2in (4cm). Various colors of upholstery fabric are used to create these exquisite tiny characters. Each one-of-a-kind bear is fully jointed with French knot eyes. *Photograph by Okiyasu Sugi.*

Harumi Sugimoto

I don't make bears for any one but me. I am getting recognized more though. I did receive third prize at the Japan Teddy Bear Convention for New Figures in the bear world.

My background is one of art, in fact I graduated from the Tama Artistic College and it was when I was very impressed with a Steiff Teddy Bear that I began creating stuffed animals, and in particular Teddy Bears. That was in 1985.

I stick to one-of-a-kind bears and rarely make more than ten rayon bears a year. The smallest bear is 10in (25cm).

It gives me so much joy to present a beautiful bear to a special friend. The pleasure and satisfaction of creating unique, elegant Teddy Bears satisfies me greatly.

283. Harumi Sugimoto's goal is to create bears with unique concepts and individuality. He holds *Cherry* gently in his right hand. She is made of brown rayon with a hand-carved wooden snout. In *Cherry*, Harumi embodies the sweetness, charm, and elegant air of a female bear. Nestled in Harumi's left arm is *Blueberry*. Harumi chooses this color of rayon to portray the warmth and pride of a father bear.

284. *Hope.* 1995. 10in (25cm); brown cotton; plastic eyes; fully jointed. The sprouting little green leaves and the lines on the paw pads are creatively designed to represent the grain of a tree. Harumi's concept is to generate a feeling of hope and new life with this bear. Limited edition of three.

Kazuko Sugimoto

I make bears entirely without patterns. And all are hand-sewn. I love Disney characters and my miniature bears frequently wear caps like that of various Disney characters.

I was inspired by Emi Koyanagi to make bears. She taught me how to make bears and work with materials.

Since I began making bears I have received several awards at Teddy Bear conventions in 1993 and 1994.

I complete about 400 bears a year all by myself. They sell anywhere from $90 to $120.

I love living in my house with all my cute little bears.

285. Kazuko Sugimoto affectionately holds one of her exquisite little bears in her hands.

286. Kazuko Sugimoto enjoys recreating well-known characters into her tiny teddy designs. Pictured are three bears dressed as the "Three Little Pigs." Each bear holds a hand puppet representing the "Big Bad Wolf." Produced in a limited edition of three sets, each bear is 2in (5cm).

136

Yukie Tatsuki
LES NOUNOURS PAR YUKIÉ

287. Yukie Tatsuki won the Grand Prize award for one of her adorable miniature bears at JTBA's 1995 convention. Yukie also makes wonderful sweet faced bears in larger sizes.

288. *Cherry Babies.* 1995. 3—4in (8—10cm); pale beige synthetic plush; glass eyes; fully jointed.

I graduated from Joshi bijutsu Daigaku (Women's College of Fine Arts) and worked at a graphic design office and later on as a freelance illustrator. My inspiration came when I started to make bears for "Jenny" (a kind of Japanese BARBIE® Doll) to hold in her arms. This was in 1993.

Since then, my classic style, miniature bears received a number of prizes at the Japan Teddy Bear Association's Third Annual Convention in 1995. These included the Grand Prize, the Gold Prize in the "miniature" category, and the Number One Popularity Prize!

One of my dreams is to write and publish a book about (of course) bears. I did so enjoy participating in the writing of the book *Watashi no Teddy Bear 4* (Nihon Vogue Sya).

I make about 50 one-of-a-kind bears a year and sell most of them in Tokyo for ¥8,000 to ¥40,000 (approximately $80 to $400). They range in size from 1-1/4—15-1/2in (3.5—40cm).

BEAR MAKING HINTS: Carefully observe live animals. This will help you more than you know.

289. (Left) *Cookie Faces.* 1995. 16in (40cm); blonde colored mohair; glass eyes; fully jointed. (Center and right) *Cookie Faces.* 1995. 4in (10cm); blonde mohair; glass eyes; fully jointed. Bears were made for the book *Watashi no Teddy Bear 4* (Nihon Vogue Sya).

290. The character Rie Watanabe incorporates into the facial and body design of her miniature bears enhances their endearing qualities.

My bears are mostly mini-ones made of mohair with hand-made accessories. Even though my bears are small, they sit down with a flop, because their stuffing is very tight and includes little grains of steel, just like big bears.

I enjoy setting the small bears with even smaller ones in my work area and constantly imagine various scenes of the bear's world.

For the past three years I have made and sold bears, and manage to complete about 200 miniature bears a year. They range in size from 2-1/2—4in (6—10cm) and I sell them for ¥7,000 to ¥20,000 ($70 to $200).

In 1993 I was honored to receive the Rosemary prize of the International Teddy Bear Exhibition here in Tokyo. You can see an example of my work in *Teddy Bear and Friends*® (No. 136). My bears are identified by the anklet with their name and my brand name.

Before long, I plan to create my own big doll house of a tiny "bear town."

I get many letters from my customers and am so pleased that my bears are loved and treasured by so many people. I was especially gladdened to hear that one lady even rescued my bears from the earthquake in Kobe.

291. *Mac.* 1995. 4in (10cm); pale cream colored mohair; black onyx beads eyes; fully jointed. Papa bear *Mac* affectionately hugs his baby.

Helen Godfrey
BUZZBEE BEARS

292. Helen Godfrey, surrounded by some of her wonderful Buzzbee Bear creations.

I named my company Buzzbee Bears because the name reminds me of buzzing bees and bears who eat honey!

My first bear was cute, but not terribly professional. I had always been curious about how bears moved, never having pulled one apart. In those days, the mid 1980s, it was impossible to get good patterns or bear supplies, so it was very frustrating.

Eventually, I made my own pattern and used what I had learned from my earlier efforts and by studying my childhood bears. I came across a factory which had several rolls of beautiful German acrylic fabric and experimented with that. One thing it did teach me was that good quality materials are essential for bear making. In fact, it makes all the difference.

It takes me about three hours to make a basic bear, with the special outfits and all. They take up a lot of time.

I truly enjoy coming up with new bear designs and having people coming back for more of my bears. And teaching brings me great rewards as well. I have taught bear making in my home at various times. I have moved fairly often in recent years, so I advertise when I plan to hold new classes.

Since 1985, more than 1000 bears have been born. They range in size from 3—12in (8—31cm). I name each one individually.

BEAR MAKING HINTS:
1. Ask non-bear collectors to tell you what they think of your bears. It is an interesting way of picking up some honest comments.
2. Experiment with shifting cardboard pattern pieces around, making sure you get the best value from the fabric.
3. Look at your bears in the mirror to help highlight the mistakes you might miss otherwise.

293 *Clown Teddy.* 1994. 6in (15cm); golden mohair head and paws; bright purple and vivid turquoise clown suit (an integral part of body); glass bead eyes; unjointed body stuffed with pellets. Comes in signed/dated box.

139

294. Syndi Muir and her daughter found a picturesque setting by the ocean to be photographed with three of Syndi's favorite bears. (Left to right) *Big Bear.* 1992. 28in (71cm). *Open Mouth* (gold medal winner). 1994. 11in (28cm). *Cuddles.* 1995. 17in (43cm).

I feel that I could be making bears every waking moment. As it is, I produce only 80 bears a year. Most are limited editions of approximately 10-20. I also do one-of-a-kinds and open editions.

It is difficult trying to explain to the general public (not people who already collect bears) that quality doesn't come by accident. It is the result of creative effort, superior materials, and artistic ability that takes years to refine!

I charge $75-$100 for 2-1/2in (6cm) disk-jointed, dressed bears; $110-$140 for 11in (28cm) mohair "ted" with antique trims and $180-$280 for 17in (43cm) mohair, pellet and poly filled bears. All of them have a sewn in tag with MUIR and the year they are made.

I sell wholesale to shops and directly to collectors and have received a bronze and gold medal at my first show (The Annual New Zealand Teddy Festival) in 1994.

BEAR MAKING HINTS:
1. When experimenting, use inexpensive materials first.
2. For stuffing big bears and tiny bears, use a wooden chopstick sanded to a blunt point.
3. If you use the eye end of a darning needle to turn and stuff the "tinies," be careful as it doesn't have as much "give" as wood and is easier to poke a hole in the fabric.

140

Robin Rive
COUNTRYLIFE NEW ZEALAND

I am slightly different than many bear artists as I have 80 people making bears with me. These 20,000 bears (annually) are exhibited in six shows and sold directly to stores in New Zealand through our own representatives; through a wholesaler in the U.K., U.S.A., and Australia, and directly to retailers in Japan, Singapore, Hong Kong, and Germany.

My original designs have their own unique look and are born of European mohair, pure wool, mohair/wool blends, and man-made fabrics. These are imported in the raw state and dressed, herbal dyed, and finished to give the bears their own unique look. Hand filling gives each bear's face its own individual character and personality.

Because we market internationally, there are two unique tasks that we face. The first is designing bears to the specific tastes of different countries. The second is setting the right price for each country. Therefore we make an enormous variety of styles and designs, mainly "vintage" style bears which sell from NZ$60 to NZ$600 (approximately $40 to $414).

My husband, Bryan, and I own historic Oakdale Farm, one of the first honey farms in New Zealand. It is the perfect setting for designing romantic, old-world bears. We plan to stage a Teddy 2000 festival at our century old home.

In dedication to New Zealand's first sight of the dawn light in 2000, I am designing an Earth Love range, part of the proceeds of which will help disadvantaged children. It will use natural materials and organically grown wool from our small farm.

295. Robin Rive and her big bruin *McNaughty* make a grand looking pair as they proudly pose for the picture. *Photograph by Bryan Rive.*

296. (Front left) *Matilda.* 1995. 12-1/2in (32cm); medium brown herbal dyed man-made fabric; natural suede paw pads; plastic safety eyes; fully jointed. The Herbal dyed fabric is actually four unique processes to give the look of antique mohair. (Front right) *Algeron.* 1994. 12-1/2in (32cm); medium brown herbal dyed manmade fabric; natural suede paw pads; plastic safety eyes; fully jointed. (Back) *Chesterton.* 1994. 17in (43cm); warm brown manmade fabric; natural suede paw pads; plastic safety eyes; fully jointed. Free standing. *Photograph by Bryan Rive.*

141

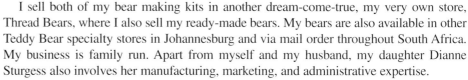

Eunice Catherine Beaton
THREAD BEARS

I made my first bear in 1984 and had such a tremendous response from my family and friends, that I started making bears for resale in 1985. Two of my latest lines are The Kalahari Collection, produced from South African Mohair and The Mopane Silk Series, produced from wild silk.

In the beginning of my bear making career it was extremely difficult to obtain any suitable supplies in Durban. Joints, eyes, and synthetic fur — not to mention mohair — were unavailable. The first animal eyes I found had to be filed to shape! My husband, Claude, devised a plan for making the joints. Cotton-rich velour was my solution for bearskins.

The difficulties I faced were a great challenge and when I decided to launch my own range of kits in 1992, I had to order a

297. Eunice Beaton, one of the pioneer Teddy Bear artists in South Africa, teaches Teddy Bear making classes and imports fabrics to inspire and generate the interest in Teddy Bear artistry in her country. Eunice also lovingly restores old Teddy Bears.

hundred meters of fabric made up to my color specifications. For a small, home-based business this was a financial risk to say the least. These kits consist of a silk-screened pattern on a cotton-velour fabric, instruction leaflet, pattern sheet, joints, eyes, embroidery thread, and a swing tag saying "I made it myself!" to hang around the neck of completed bears. I use this kit in my classes, specifically for first-time bear makers. It is also very well received on a national basis by women in the country areas who aren't able to attend classes, but who had basic sewing skills and were keen to make their own bears.

The Bearton Range was my first kit. I launched a new range in March, 1995. Called the Country Collection, it differs in both design and fabric as my intention is to introduce a synthetic fur for bear makers. I joined with a local manufacturer who produced four different synthetic fur fabrics to my specifications.

For me, a dream-come-true has been the realization of a truly South African produced mohair which is suitable for bearmaking. I developed this fabric in collaboration with the Council for Scientific and Industrial Research and it has taken a lot of time, effort, and trial-and-error experiments to achieve what I feel is a unique textile.

I sell both of my bear making kits in another dream-come-true, my very own store, Thread Bears, where I also sell my ready-made bears. My bears are also available in other Teddy Bear specialty stores in Johannesburg and via mail order throughout South Africa. My business is family run. Apart from myself and my husband, my daughter Dianne Sturgess also involves her manufacturing, marketing, and administrative expertise.

My daughter organizes The Annual Teddy Bear and Doll Fair where I present my bears each year. I also participate in the knitting and craft workshop. I produce an average of 200 traditional and more contemporarily designed bears each year.

My small (9in {23cm}) limited edition, cotton-velour, or mohair bears sell for between SA Rand 80 to 130 (approximately $23 to $37); the medium limited edition, mohair bears (10—16in {25—40cm}) sell for between SA Rand 130 to 350 (approximately $37 to $100); and my large (16in {40cm}) limited edition mohair bears sell from SA Rand 350 (approximately $100) and more.

BEAR MAKING HINTS: To prevent the fur from extending out of the seam allowance whilst stitching the bear shapes together, tuck the fur to the inside of the shape and, using small pins, position the pins parallel to the very edge of the fabric. Using a 6mm seam allowance, the machine foot simply glides over the pins as you stitch. It does not matter if the pins are positioned on the top or underneath and they need not be removed until all the stitching has been completed.

298. *Bo.* 1995. 23-3/4in (60cm); brown distressed mohair (manufactured in South Africa); glass eyes; fully jointed. The design of this bear is based on the Bushman of the Kalahari. He is appropriately attired in leather loin cloth (beaded) carrying a bow and quiver in a leather bag slung over his shoulder. This bear was created as a prototype and a smaller version will be available in a limited edition of 40. *Photograph by Rod Bathfield.*

Karin Koller & René Tscherrig
PINK DINO BEARS

299. René Tscherring (left) and Karin Koller (right) with an array of their adorable bear designs.

We went to England for our holidays and on the second day we found a Teddy Bear shop with artist bears. We totally fell in love with these bears and the rest of the time we were hunting for bears with the British Teddy Bear Guide in our hands. We couldn't find any. So, one boring Sunday afternoon, Karin took some plush and began to make her first bear. We liked it very much. That was the beginning of our Teddy Bear career.

As we like the American artist bears so much, we try to give our bears a similar look, like long arms and legs. We make all different sizes and colors.

Perhaps it sounds funny to you, but I think our bears are the ones who dictate how they look — not we! We ask the bear what his ears should look like; if he wants to smile or to look sad; if he wants long arms and legs or if he likes to be small and fat. I think it is very hard to make a bear if you can't talk with him. I'm quite sure the bear won't live if you can't speak with him and he will be just a toy.

Bear making is like a drug. We work nine hours a day in an office. Then, we come back home and sit down and make our bears until midnight or even later. The bears in our heads just want to be produced. Maybe we are a little bit crazy. But we are happy, and that's better than the things you can hear and see every day in the news.

Karin and I make our own bears from head to toe. Sometimes we help each other with the joints or eyes. We sell our bears at a monthly craft shows and at some doll fairs. Last year we made five doll shows (there are no bear shows in Switzerland). We made around 100 bears for sale and 30 or 40 just for us! We really don't like this thing with numbers. Normally we make three to seven bears of the same kind, but don't sell them as limited editions. All of our bears are signed on the foot, and they get a pink wooden sign with the Pink Dino on it.

Smaller bears (6in {15cm}) go for 80-100 Swiss-Francs (approximately $73 to $100); a bigger one (12-5/8in {30 cm}) will be around 150 Swiss-Francs (approximately $135). The most expensive is around 400 Swiss-Francs (approximately $359).

300. *Ueli.* 1994. 10in (25cm); gold mohair; glass eyes; fully jointed. *Ueli's* happy expression depicts his pleasure at the country setting René chose for him among the rustic handmade wooden cows.

The magical fairy bears of talented Japanese artist Michi Takahashi are recreated in this exquisite Premier Edition figurine, *Fairy Chuckle*. You'll fall in love with the two diminutive teddies nestled in fragile flower petals. These petite blue and pink companions follow the Japanese custom of politely covering their mouths when laughing. Released April 1996. Item #X5137. $17.95

Figurines Available from
Hobby House Press
1-800-554-1447

Second in the Teddy Bear Artist Figurine Series is a miniature rendition of world-famous American bear artist Joan Woessner's 1995 Walt Disney® World's Teddy Bear Auction piece, *On a Sunday Drive*. The one-of-a-kind plush version commanded $3,200 at the auction. Every elegant aspect of the Victorian costumes draping these superb bears are sculpted into this uniquely collectible figurine.

INTERNATIONAL TEDDY BEAR ARTIST FIGURINES

Figurines are the latest Teddy Bear collectible to capture the market's interest. This new chapter of the Teddy Bear story is rapidly becoming a best seller. These miniature works of art are quickly finding their way into the hearts and collections of today's bear world. To enhance existing Teddy Bear collections and to add to the value of Teddy Bear artists plush versions, there is now the opportunity to own darling, hand-crafted miniature renditions of unique bears originally created by famous artists.

For many years I admired many other popular figurine designers and manufacturers. This is why Hobby House Press and I are particularly proud to announce the introduction of a series of Teddy Bear figurines modeled after full-sized counterparts designed by internationally acclaimed Teddy Bear artists. Each miniature ceramic figure comes with its own story, a certificate of authenticity, a short biography and a photograph of the original artist.

The series are diminutive reproductions of the work of famous bears artists from around the world. Each collectible figurine is sculpted and painstakingly hand-painted by skilled artisans.

Our first series features three artists you can find in my first book, *Tribute to Teddy Bear Artists*. The Premier Edition is designed by Michi Takahashi (Fairy Chuckle, Japan). Wonderful collectible figurines by Joan Woessner (Bear Elegance Exclusives, America); and Rosalie Frischmann (Mill Creek Exclusives, America) will be releases two and three.

The International Teddy Bear Artist Figurine Series is proud to present Rosalie Frischmann's appealing, child-like creations as the third part of the ongoing line. These adorable bears, which brought Rosalie so much attention, will be available in this new, smaller format, exact to the last darling detail.

OTHER BOOKS BY THE AUTHOR:

CREATING HEIRLOOM TEDDY BEARS
AMERICAN TEDDY BEAR ENCYCLOPEDIA
TEDDY BEAR ARTISTS POSTCARDS
TRIBUTE TO TEDDY BEAR ARTISTS
4TH TEDDY BEAR & FRIENDS® PRICE GUIDE
TEDDY BEARS PAST & PRESENT, VOLUME I
TEDDY BEARS PAST & PRESENT, VOLUME II
THE RAIKES BEAR & DOLL STORY (*Revised Edition*)
TEDDY BEAR MEN

TEDDY BEAR ARTIST INDEX

Provided is an alphabetical list of artists divided into countries within the book. Addresses were accurate as of completion of the manuscript. Many Teddy Bear artists work out of their homes and as such do not encourage walk-in business. Please write to artists to ascertain how you can see their complete range of designs.

AMERICAN TEDDY BEAR ARTISTS

Lori Baker.................9
L. Baker and Co.
1540 New Gambier Road
Mt. Vernon, OH 43050

Jody Battaglia..........10
beary best friends
1603 Exeter Court
Marietta, GA 30068

Wendy Brent............11
1043 University #249
San Diego, CA 92103

Deanna Brittsan 12
Bears By Deanna
Brittsan
1155 Uppingham Drive
Thousand Oaks, CA
91360

Jean Burhans 13
Critters
7936 Serene Street
Brooksville, FL 34613

Renee Casey 14
Renee's Bears and
Other Things
11245 183rd St. Suite
170
Cerritos, CA 90703

Allen Chau 15
Whatabear
P.O. Box 3461
Seal Beach, CA 90740

Susan Coe 16
Bear Feet
148 Fowler Drive
Monrovia, CA 91016

Wanda Cole..............17
Forever Oregon Bears
2545 Cubit Street
Eugene, OR 97402

Pam Collins-White..18
The Toymaker
RR 2 Box 5070
Union, ME 04862

Anne Cranshaw 19
E. Willoughby Bear Co.
2 Star Road
Cape Elizabeth, ME
04107

Rhoda Curtis 20
Reminder Shop
742 Melody Lane
Edmonds, WA 98028

Sandra Dineen 21
Sandy's Bearly Bruins
11 Huntington Court
Toms River, NJ 08753

Luwana Eldredge....22
Kare 'N' Love Bears
'Future Antiques'
1140 Fern Street
Escondido, CA 92027

Kimberly Fischer 23
Kimberly's Bearied
Treasure

1 Central Avenue &
West Broadway
Haledon, NJ 07508

Robin Foley 24
Rag-O-Muffins
2917 SW Fairview
Road
Portland, OR 97201

Marsha Friesen 26
Friends Forever
2467 Fairview Road
American Falls, ID
83211

Pat Fye.....................27
Pat Fye Originals
434 Platina Drive
Diamond Bar, CA
91765

Barbara Garrett 28
BG Bears
9525 Feeg Court
Manassas, VA 22110

Mary George............29
Mary George Bears
46713 Camelia Drive
Canton, MI 48187

Barbara Golden 30
Can't Bear To Part
3932 Digby Court #10
Richmond, VA 23233

Frances Harper 31
Apple of My Eye
233 Main Avenue
South Hampton, NH
03827

Terry Hayes..............32
Pendleton's Teddy
Bears
2447 Skidmore Road
Greensburg, PA 15601

Claire Herz 33
Capricious Creatures
P.O. Box 622
Montclair, NJ 07042

Beth Diane Hogan ..34
Some Bears and Other
Beasts
5629 N. Bonfair Avenue
Lakewood, CA 90712

Susan Horn 35
Susan Horn Bears

Debbie Kesling 36
Bears by Debbie Kesling
8429 Lambert Drive
Lambertville, MI 48144

Barbara King 37
Barbara King Bears
1553 Ridgeway Drive
Glendale, CA 91202

Kathy LacQuay 38
Bearskins

845 La Salle Place
St. Cloud, MN 56301

Denzil Laurence 39
Personalized Theme
Teddy Bears by Denzil
1118 W. Magnolia
Burbank, CA 91506

Tammie Lawrence ..40
Tammie's Teddy's
717 Dakota
Holton, KS 66436

Rose Leshko 41
Bear Valley Bears

Rita Loeb.................42
Rita Loeb's Tiny Teddy
Company
2995 Van Buren Bl.
#A13-145
Riverside, CA 92503

Tracy Main 43
Teddys by Tracy
32 Pikehall Pl.
Baltimore, MD 21236

Diane L. Martin 44
Blue Moon Bears
5665 Azalea Circle
Pollock Pines, CA
95726

Randy Martin, Sr. ..45
Lil' Brother's Bears
3212 135th Street
Toledo, OH 43611

Heidi Miller..............46
Lovins & Huggybears
404 Louisiana Avenue
Libby, MT 59923

Bonnie H. Moose 47
Bears, Hares and Other
Wares
500 W. 33rd Street
Baltimore, MD 21211

**Roger and Helen
Morris 48**
Factoria Toy Works
12203 SE 35th Street
Bellevue, WA 98006

Cecilia Moudree 49
Zoolatana Bear Co.
2808 Kootenai
Boise, ID 83705

Pat Murphy..............49
Murphy Bears
6900 Jennings Road
Ann Arbor, MI 48105

Kathy Myers.............50
You Need A Bear By
Kathy Myers
20902 Cortner Avenue
Lakewood, CA 90715-
1661

Sue Newlin 51
Sue Newlin Originals
519 South 5th Avenue
Arcadia, CA 91006

**Beverly Matteson
Port 52**
Beverly Port Originals
Box 711
Retsil, WA 98378

John Paul Port 54
Van Poort Designs
c/o Paul's Pharmacy
732 Lebo Blvd.
Bremerton, WA 98310

Kimberlee Port........55
Kimberlee Port
Originals
P.O. Box 85534
Seattle, WA 98145

**Olwyn and William
Price 56**
Wil-O-Wyn
103 Cass Avenue
Atlantic, IA 50022

**Michelle Province-
Gesher 57**
Itty Bitty Small
Originals & Pattern Co,
3116 Thorn Street
San Diego, CA 92104-
4618

**Susan Redstreake
Geary 58**
New Mexico Bear Paws
Trueman Court
Baltimore, MD 21244

Monty & Joe Sours..59
The Bear Lady
Route 1, Box 40
Golden City, MO 64748

M. Michele Thorp ..61
Mossy Log Studio
36910 Edgehill Road
Springfield, OR 97478

ConnieTognoli..........62
Connie's Bears and
Bunnies
1415 El Nido Drive
Fallbrook, CA 92028

Julia Watada 63
Watada Designs
1320 Whipple Avenue
Redwood City, CA
94062

Robert Welch 15
Whatabear
P.O. Box 3461
Seal Beach, CA 90740

Mary Ann Wills 64
P.O. Box 542
Aldie, VA 22001

Janet Wilson 64
Handmade Treasures
22 Sally Ann Court
Stewartstown, PA 17363

Joyce Yates 66
Bearly Victorian
6121 Queens Brigade
Court
Fairfax, VA 22030

Barbara Zimmerman ..67
Zimm's Bears and
Hares
4521 Timbery Drive
Jefferson, MD 21755

Marie Zimmermann ..68
Paw Quette Bears
251 Van Bee Drive
Willam Bay, WI 53191

AUSTRALIAN TEDDY BEAR ARTISTS

Linda Benson 69
Benson Bears
P.O. Box 251
Kurrajong NSW 2758
Australia

Samantha Fredericks..70
Bliss Toys
9 Lancaster Ave.
Newton VIC 3220
Australia

Ronwyn Graham 71
Bambini Design
P.O. Box 18
East Bentleigh VIC
3165
Australia

Loris Hancock 72
Studio SeventySuite
370/80
"The Pines" Shopping
Centre
Elanora, QLD 4223
Australia

Lexie Haworth 73
Bears of Haworth
Cottage
7 Walsh Crescent
North Nowra NSW 2540
Australia

Sonja Heron 74
Heartfelt Bears
13 Aqueduct Avenue
Mt. Evelyn
Melbourne Victoria
3796
Australia

Marianne Howe 75
Omi's Bears
P.O. Box 38
Franklin TAS 7113
Australia

**Michelle and Julie
Hyland....................76**
Hyland Bears
P.O. Box 16
Kalamunda, WA 6076
Australia

Jennifer Laing 77
Totally Bear
6 Walter Road
Ingleside, Sydney NSW
2101
Australia

Cindy McDonald 78
Jumbuck Bears
P.O. Box 896
Mudgee NSW 2850
Australia

Rosalie MacLeman 79
MacBears
Woodstock on Loddon
RSB TISW 3539 VIC
Australia

Carole Marshall......80
Balmain Bear
41 Wortley Street
Balmain, Sidney NSW
2041
Australia

Denise Matthews 81
Denise and Friends
Original Bears
P.O. Box 203
Diamond Creek
MelbourneVIC 3089
Australia

Briony Nottage........81
The House of Brooke-
Bri
451 Henley Beach
Road
Lockleys, South
Australia 5032
Australia

Debbie Sargenston..83
Nostalgia Bears-
Australia
44 Ivanhoe Grove
Chadstone, Melbourne
3148
Australia

Kay vanderLey 84
Completely Stu'd
204 Crotty's Lane
Kempsey NSW 2440
Australia

AUSTRIAN TEDDY BEAR ARTISTS

Karin Kronsteiner ..85
Kunstlerbaren
Krenngasse 8 A-8010
Graz
Austria

145

146

TEDDY BEAR ARTIST BEAR PRICE GUIDE

This index includes the current value of artist bears illustrated in this book. Please refer to illustration number for picture of bears.

AMERICAN TEDDY BEAR ARTISTS

Illustration	Name of Artist	Company Name	Name of Bear	Year	Size	Price $
9	Lori Ann Baker	L. Baker and Co.	Pinocchio	1995	19in (48cm)	$200.
11	Jody A. Battaglia	beary best friends	Susie Gumdrop	1995	7in (18cm)	$80.
13	Wendy Brent		Lord Bluestone	1995	22in (56cm)	$370.
15	Deanna Brittsan	Bears By Deanna Brittsan	Buckles	1993	13in (33cm)	$175.
17	Jean Burhan's	Critters	The Family Stroll	1995	6-19in (15-48cm)	$475. (set)
19	Renee & Jim Casey	Renee's Bears and Other Things	Victorian Pin Cushion Teddies	1995		$95. each
23	Sue Coe	Bear Feet	Nikki	1994	7in (18cm)	$95.
25	Wanda Cole	Forever Oregon Bears	Shadow	1995	18in (46cm)	$499.
27	Pam Collins-White	The Toymaker	Boomer Raccoon	1993	24in (61cm)	$540.
	Pam Collins-White	The Toymaker	Bing Bear	1987	10in (25cm)	$65.
29	Anne Cranshaw	E. Willoughby Bear Company	Ebearneezer Scrooge	1992	18in (46cm)	$500.
35	Luwana Eldredge	Kare 'N' Love Bears 'Future Antiques'	Jester Bears	1995	2-12in (5-31cm)	$75.- $275.
37	Kimberly Fischer	Kimberly's Bearied Treasure®	Applesauce (Bear)	1995	23in (58cm)	$495. (set)
			Porkchops (Pig)	1995	11in (28cm)	
38	Kimberly Fischer	Kimberly's Bearied Treasure®	Tundra (Bear)	1994	25in (64cm)	$895. (set)
			Peep (Penguin)	1994	14in (36cm)	
39	Robin Foley	Rag-O-Muffins	Orion	1995	20in (51cm)	$900.
40	Robin Foley	Rag-O-Muffins	Anna Korrina	1995	20in (51cm)	$900.
42	Marsha Friesen	Friends Forever	Goat-Billy	1995	48in (122cm)	$1,000.
43	Marsha Friesen	Friends Forever	Grandma Hattie &	1993	25in (64cm)	$580. (set)
			Little Mugsy	1993	12in (31cm)	
47	Barbara Garrett	BG Bears	Peter Pan	1994	3in (8cm)	$120.
			Hook	1994	4in (10cm)	$130.
			Tinkerbell	1994	1in (3cm)	$120.
			Wendy	1994	3-1/4in (9cm)	$120.
			Michael	1994	3in (8cm)	$120.
			John	1994	2-1/4in (6cm)	$130.
48	Barbara Garrett	BG Bears	Geppetto &	1994	4in (10cm)	$260. (set)
			Pinocchio (Puppet & Puppetmaster)		3in (8cm)	
50	Mary George	Mary George Bears	Old German Bears	1995	20-23in (51-58cm)	$275.-$395.
51	Barbara Golden	Can't Bear To Part	Bruin	1994	14in (36cm)	$170.
52	Barbara Golden	Can't Bear To Part	Tweedledee and Tweedledum	1995	16in (14cm)	$600. (set)
53	Barbara Golden	Can't Bear To Part	The Mad Hatter	1995	14in (36cm)	$195.
55	Frances Harper	Apple of My Eye	Nicky	1995	12in (31cm)	$120.
			Nicoletta	1995	19in (48cm)	$210.
57	Terry Hayes	Pendleton's Teddy Bears	Scrappy	1995	9in (23cm)	$85.
58	Claire Herz	Capricious Creatures	The Hatmaker		9in (23cm)	
59	Claire Herz	Capricious Creatures	Nokeo		13in (33cm)	
			Hicoray		6in (15cm)	
61	Beth Diane Hogan	Some Bears and Other Beasts	Old Heartbeat	1994	2in (5cm)	$100.
			Leopard	1995	2in (5cm)	$165.
			Fred	1995	3in (8cm)	$95.
63	Susan Horn	Susan Horn Bears	Natalie & Naughty (the puppy)	1994	16in (41cm)	$395. (set)
65	Debbie Kesling	Bears by Debbie Kesling	Clown Purse Necklace	1994	2-1/2in (6cm)	$250.
69	Kathy LacQuay	Bearskins	Running Bear	1992	2-3/4in (7cm)	$150.
			Little White Dove	1994	2-3/4in (7cm)	$120.
71	Denzil Laurence	Personalized Theme Teddy Bears by Denzil	Bishop Bear	1995	15in (38cm)	$250.
73	Tammie Lawrence	Tammie's Teddys	Alphonse	1994	16in (41cm)	$400.
			Elouise	1995	16in (41cm)	$400.
74	Tammie Lawrence	Tammie's Teddys	Gardening	1994-1995	9in (23cm)	$185.
			Genevieve Rabbit	1994-1995	9in (23cm)	$185.
			Earnestina Eggbasket	1994-1995	9in (23cm)	$185.
			Primrose Panda	1994-1995	9in (23cm)	$185.
76	Rose Leshko	Bear Valley Bears	Heather	1995	18in (46cm)	$175.
			Winston	1995	24in (61cm)	$250.
78	Rita Loeb	Rita Loeb's Tiny Teddy Company	P.J. Jammy Bear	1993	2-2-1/2in (5-6cm)	$85.
80	Tracy Main	Teddys by Tracy	Bears	1995	3/4-2-1/2in (2-6cm)	$30.- $45.
82	Diane L. Martin	Blue Moon Bears	Sophie (sitting) Emily (standing)	1995	13in (33cm)	$150 (each)
84	Randy Martin	Lil' Brother's Bears	King Penguin (Baby)	1995	1-1/2in (4cm)	$225. (set)
			and King Penguin (Adult)	1995	1-7/8in (4cm)	
			Giant (Tiny) Panda	1995	2in (5cm)	$125.
86	Heidi Miller	Lovins & Huggybears	Chinook Saves the Christmas Seal	1993	28in (71cm)	$1,000. (set)
88	Bonnie H. Moose	Bears, Hares and Other Wares	Ruggles and Rigsby	1995	9-23in (23-58cm)	$250. (set)
89	Bonnie Moose & Susan Redstreake Geary	Bears Hares and Other Wares & New Mexico Bear Paws	Laverne and Shirley Go for a Spin	1995	1-1/4-11-3/4in (3-30cm)	$550. (set)
94	Pat Murphy	Murphy Bears	Keanu	1994	15in (38cm)	$195.
			Rusty	1994	20in (51cm)	$260.
96	Kathy Myers	You Need A Bear By Kathy Myers	Little LilliAnn	1993-1996	9-1/2in (20cm)	$150.
			Mandy Panda	1993-1996	6in (15cm)	$195.
			Simone	1993	3in (8cm)	$150.
			Cubby	1994	8in (20cm)	$150.
98	Sue Newlin	Sue Newlin Originals	Henry	1995	22in (56cm)	$230.
			Sawyer	1992	18in (46cm)	$198.
			Scotty	1991	15in (38cm)	$168.
			Old Sonny	1994	8-1/2in (22cm)	$88.
100	Beverly Matteson Port	Beverly Port Originals	Tedwina Cinnabär	1974-1995	14in (35cm)	$695.
			Baby Brat	1975-1995	4in (10cm)	$350.
			Tiny Tedwina	1974-1995	3in (8cm)	$295.

Illustration	Name of Artist	Company Name	Name of Bear	Year	Size	Price $
102	The Port Family		Theodore B Bear	1974-1995	15in (38cm)	$695.
			Sarafina Sunflower Bearkin	1978-1995	14in (36cm)	$595.
			Olde RememBear	1960	8in (20cm)	$150.
	John Paul Port		Lucky Rainbow	1994	12in (31cm)	$85.
	Kimberlee Port		Shimmer E. Rainbow	1991	3in (8cm)	$395.
104	John Paul Port	Van Poort Designs	Mr. Bumbles	1995	12in (30cm)	$135.
105	John Paul Port	Van Poort Designs	Hansl	1990	21in (53cm)	$500.
			Beartl	1990	21in (53cm)	$500.
108	Kimberlee Port	Kimberlee Port Originals	Roosevelt	1994	5in (13cm)	$450.
110	Olwyn & William Price	Wil-O-Wyn Bears	Tedman Lovewell	1994	18in (46cm)	$1,200.
112	Michelle Province-Gesher	Itty Bitty Small Originals & Pattern Co.	Bumble Bear	1994	3-1/2in (9cm)	$125.
			Piggin's	1995	2-1/2in (6cm)	$100.
			Tug	1995	4-3/8in (11cm)	$150.
			Emmett	1995	1-7/8in (5cm)	$100.
113	Susan Redstreake Geary	New Mexico Bear Paws	Carly	1993	15in (38cm)	$225.
114	Susan Redstreake Geary & Bonnie Moose	New Mexico Bear Paws and Bears, Hares and Other Wares	Love is More Precious When Given Away	1995	27in (69cm)	$1,000. (set)
115	Monty and Joe Sours	The Bear Lady	Jackie	1993	12in (30cm)	$2,500.
			Horace Eugene	1994	15in (38cm)	$3,500.
118	Monty and Joe Sours	The Bear Lady	Albert	1993	18in (46cm)	$350.
			Waldo	1993	14in (36cm)	$250.
			Christopher	1993	10in (25cm)	$150.
120	M. Michele Thorp	Mossy Log Studio	Cornpone and His Prize Winning Pig Sou-ee	1993	16in (41cm)	$395. (set)
122	Connie Tognoli	Connie's Bears and Bunnies	Bearly Christmas Santa Doll & Bears	1986	20in (51cm)	$1,200. (set)
123	Connie Tognoli	Connie's Bears and Bunnies	Special Crayon Delivery	1995	4-1/2in (12cm) by 10in (25cm)	$225. (set)
125	Julie Watada	Watada Designs	Ballerina Bear	1989	1-3/4in (5cm)	$135.
			Dressed Holiday Bear	1992	2in (5cm)	$195.
			Dressed Bear	1995	2in (5cm)	$135.
			Mini Bo Bear	1990	3in (8cm)	$95.
			Stamp Size Teddy	1995	1-1/2in (4cm)	$85.
			Blond Bear	1990	3in (8cm)	$95.
			Bear In Red Shirt	1994	1-5/8in (4cm)	$95.
128	Janet Wilson	Handmade Treasures	Sprinkles	1994	3in (8cm)	$135.
129	Janet Wilson	Handmade Treasures	Wynken, Blynken, and Nod	1993	2-3/8in (6cm)	$750. (set)
130	Joyce Yates	"Bearly Victorian"	Baby Christina	1994	20in (51cm)	$450.
			Lady Thornbeary	1995	18in (46cm)	$325.
			Gwendolyn Fareday	1994	15in (38cm)	$225.
132	Barbara Zimmerman	Zimm's Bears and Hares	Abbot	1995	10-1/2in (27cm)	$110.
			Dan Dee	1995	24in (61cm)	$350.
134	Marie Zimmermann	Paw Quette Bears	Cherry Blossom	1995	16in (41cm)	$185.

AUSTRALIAN TEDDY BEAR ARTISTS

Illustration	Name of Artist	Company Name	Name of Bear	Year	Size	Price $
136	Linda Benson	Benson Bears	Three brothers	1995	17in (43cm)	$151. (each)
137	Samantha Fredericks	Bliss Toys	Delores	1995	10in (25cm)	$190.
			Tim Lion	1995	11in (28cm)	$190.
			Carl	1995	13in (33cm)	$200.
138	Samantha Fredericks	Bliss Toys	Adelaide	1995	10in (25cm)	$190.
			Bonnie	1995	10in (25cm)	$190.
			Delores	1995	10in (25cm)	$190.
140	Ronwyn Graham	Bambini Design	Magician	1993	3-3/8in (9cm)	$136.
142	Loris Hancock	Studio Seventy	Hi Ho! Honey Bear	1995	3-4-1/2in (8-12cm)	$200. (set)
144	Lexie Haworth	Bears of Haworth Cottage	John	1995	24in (61cm)	$401.
146	Sonya Heron	Heartfelt Bears	Little Bear Blue	1995	4-1/4in (11cm)	$342.
148	Marianne Howe	Omi's Bears	Bruny	1995	5-1/2in (14cm)	$125.
150	Michelle and Julie Hyland	Hyland Bears	Blackbeard the Pirate	1994	20in (51cm)	$600.
152	Jennifer Laing	Totally Bear	Broome With Alice Springs the Kangaroo	1993	7-8in (18-20cm)	$1,400. (set)
154	Cindy McDonald	Jumbuck Bears	Torvill and Dean	1994	18in (46cm)	$570. (set)
155	Rosalie MacLeman	MacBears	Boomer	1994	16in (41cm)	$753.
156	Rosalie MacLeman	MacBears	Willie	1995	19in (48cm)	$753.
158	Carole Marshall	Balmain Bear	Walter	1994	20in (51cm)	$250.
			Bubby	1995	9in (23cm)	$60.
161	Briony Nottage	The House of Brooke-Bri	Kanga	1993	12in (31cm)	$175.
			B.B. Bear	1995	10in (25cm)	$95.
162	Briony Nottage	The House of Brooke-Bri	Fiske	1995	10in (25cm)	$300. (each)
164	Debbie Sargentson	Nostalgia Bears-Australia	Marmaduke and Marmaduke Junior	1994	10-24in (25-61cm)	$452. (set)
166	Kay vander Ley	Completely Stu'd	Buz	1994	16in (41cm)	$15.

BELGIAN TEDDY BEAR ARTISTS

Illustration	Name of Artist	Company Name	Name of Bear	Year	Size	Price $
171	Lilian Vandepaepeliere	Lily Bear Belgium	Bear	1995	15-3/4in (40cm)	$195.

148

BRITISH TEDDY BEAR ARTISTS

Illustration	Name of Artist	Company Name	Name of Bear	Year	Size	Price $
175	John and Maude Blackburn	Canterbury Bears Limited	Baby Joshua	1995	10in (26cm)	$90.
			George		29in (74cm)	
177	Penny Chalmers	Little Charmers	Barney Winson	1994	40in (102cm)	$924.
			Bugle	1994	14in (36cm)	$270.
			Badger	1994	18in (46cm)	$270.
180	Janet Clark	Teddystyle	Unity	1994	20-48in (51-112cm)	$1,847. (set)
182	Doreen Frankham	Wee Growlers and Belly Button Bears	Bearlock Holmes	1994	4-1/2in (12cm)	$140.
			Red Riding Hood	1995	3-1/2in (9cm)	$95.
			Phantom of the O'Beara	1994	4-1/2in (12cm)	$140.
184	Amanda Heugh		Fircone	1994	11in (28cm)	$200.
			Geraint	1993	16in (41cm)	$300.
			Hendre	1995	19-1/2in (50cm)	$399.
			Oliwen	1993	14in (36cm)	$254.
186	Jill Hussey	Something's Bruin	Tattered and Torn	1995	6-20in (15-51cm)	$306. (set)
190	Elaine Lonsdale	Companion Bears	Myself for Bed/	1995		
			Girl		8in (20cm)	$208.
			Boy		8in (20cm)	$208.
			Little girl		5in (13cm)	$200.
191	Elaine Lonsdale	Companion Bears	Animal Farm/	1995		$416. (set)
			Will	1995	5-1/2in (14cm)	
			Martha	1995	5-1/2in (14cm)	
194	Louise Peers		Easter Parade	1995	2-1/2in (6cm)	$246.
			Fizzy	1995	2in (5cm)	$116.
196	Katherine R. Rabjohn	Calico Bears	Friends of Fur	1994	2-1/2in (6cm)	$146.
197	Teresa Rowe	Waifs and Strays	The Honey Thief	1995	25in (64cm)	$693.
198	Teresa Rowe	Waifs and Strays	Baggins and Boo	1995	3-1/2-9in (9-23cm)	$539. (set)
			Jack In-A-Box			
			Pee-Wee	1995	8in (23cm)	$131.
			Billy Bramley		12in (31cm)	$185.
			Rambling Rose		8in (23cm)	$151.
			Tommy Tadpole		12in (31cm)	$208.
200	Sandra Wickenden	Wickenden Bears	Bear Cub	1995	20in (51cm)	$539.
			Bruin	1994	13in (33cm)X17in (43cm)	$377.
202	Carolyn Willis		Genie on Magic Carpet	1994	2-1/2in (6cm)	$308.

CANADIAN TEDDY BEAR ARTISTS

Illustration	Name of Artist	Company Name	Name of Bear	Year	Size	Price $
204	Patricia Gye	Wayfarer Bears	Otis	1995	21in (53cm)	$240.
			Otis Major	1995	23in (58cm)	$335.
206	Linda Harris	Beariations	Sunday's Child	1994	9-17in (23-43cm)	$487. (set)
207	Debi Hill	Wannabee Bears	Honey	1995	15in (38cm)	$195.
			Birdie	1995	9in (23cm)	$135.
			Howard	1995	12in (31cm)	$155.
			Nobbs	1995	23in (58cm)	$250.
			Silly Dilly	1995	9in (23cm)	$175.
208	Debi Hill	Wannabee Bears	Gollie's Ted	1995	14in (36cm)	$195.
			Vintage Gollie	1994	14in (36cm)	$165.
			Ebeegosh	1995	5in (13cm)	$125.
209	Jane Perala	Hemer House Designs	Redfurred	1995	23in (58cm)	$295.
210	Jane Perala	Hemer House Designs	Tasha	1995	12-1/2in (32cm)	$165.
212	Cheryl Schmidt	It Bears Repeating	Foam on the Range	1995	7-1/2in (19cm)	$200.
214	Trudy Yelland	Tru's Bearables	Old Friends	1994	4in (10cm)	$145.
215	Trudy Yelland	Tru's Bearables	T.R. Teddy Roosevelt	1991	4in (10cm)	$145.

DANISH TEDDY BEAR ARTIST

Illustration	Name of Artist	Company Name	Name of Bear	Year	Size	Price $
217	Grethe Olesen	Vest Wood Bears	Buddy	1995	8in (20cm)	$153.

DUTCH TEDDY BEAR ARTISTS

Illustration	Name of Artist	Company Name	Name of Bear	Year	Size	Price $
220	Marjoleine Diemel-van Rijn	Old Time Teddy's	Ashley	1995	17-1/2in (45cm)	$316.
			Joshua	1995	8-1/2in (22cm)	$95.
221	Jane Humme	Jane Humme Original Bears	Dominic	1995	20in (50cm)	$335.
			Thomas	1995	14-1/2in (38cm)	$250.
222	Jane Humme	Jane Humme Original Bears	Lotje	1994	10-1/2in (26cm)	$190.
			Lars	1994	12in (30cm)	$200.
			Mitch	1994	4-1/2in (11cm)	$120.
224	Annemieke Koetse	Boefje Bears	Jutter	1995	11in (28cm)	$240.
225	Annemieke Koetse	Boefje Bears	Bibber	1995	11in (28cm)	$240.
229	Yvonne Plakké	Yvonne Plakké Originals	Swimpy	1995	9-1/2in (24cm)	$140.
231	Lèon Romans van Schaik	Hugable Bears	Mum and Bebe	1995	9-3/4in (25cm)	$292. (set)
233	Audie F. Sison	A Teddy . . . by Audie	Casimir	1995	24in (61cm)	$550.
237	Dimph van Gemert	Skinle Bear	Isodorus	1992	8in (22cm)	$129.

Illustration	Name of Artist	Company Name	Name of Bear	Year	Size	Price $
237	Dimph van Gemert	Skinle Bear	Casper	1993	10in (26cm)	$138.
			Frederick	1993	10in (26cm)	$138.
			L'automne	1994	10in (26cm)	$200.
			Ferdinand	1994	4in (11cm)	$89.
			Eduard	1994	9in (21cm)	$89.
239	Vera van Oeveren	O'Family Collectibles	Tilly and rabbit Floortje	1995	15-1/2in (40cm)	$450. (set)
			Henry and William	1995	10-1/2in (24cm)	$185. (each)
			Harold	1995	16-3/4in (40cm)	$400.

FRENCH TEDDY BEAR ARTISTS

Illustration	Name of Artist	Company Name	Name of Bear	Year	Size	Price $
241	Aline Cousin	My Bear To Me	Berlingot	1994	19-1/2in (50cm)	$250.
			Pierrot	1994	4in (10cm)	$100.
			Muzo	1992	10in (25cm)	$150.
243	Marylou Jouet	JoueTeddy	Crocsou	1995	6-5/8in (17cm)	$280.

GERMAN TEDDY BEAR ARTISTS

Illustration	Name of Artist	Company Name	Name of Bear	Year	Size	Price $
245	Ulrike Amadori	Die Werkstatt	Old Henry	1995	20-1/2in (52cm)	$270.
			Jonny	1995	11-3/4in (30cm)	$160.
			Hans	1995	13-1/2in (34cm)	$170.
			Jossi	1995	6in (15cm)	$80.
248	Marie Robischon	Robin der Bär, Creation Marie	Leather Bears	1994-1995	17in (44cm)	$850.
249	Marie Robischon	Robin der Bär, Creation Marie	Oldie	1995	17in (43cm)	$980.
250	Marie Robischon	Robin der Bär, Creation Marie	Pirate	1995	17-1/4in (44cm)	$1,400.
252	Dagmar Strunck	Bärenhohle Der Teddyladen	Uliz the Colorful Bear	1995	31-1/2in (80cm)	$1,200.

JAPANESE TEDDY BEAR ARTISTS

Illustration	Name of Artist	Company Name	Name of Bear	Year	Size	Price $
261	Kazuko Ichikawa		Angie	1994	8-1/2in (22cm)	$200.
			Topy	1994	8-1/2in (22cm)	$200.
			Papu	1994	5in (13cm)	$120.
			Marshmellow	1994	9-3/4in (25cm)	$200.
263	Atsuko Isaji	Beary Tales	Strawberry	1995		$70.
			Cinnamon	1995		$120.
267	Emi Koyanagi	Needle Mama	Two Faced Bear	1994	2in (6cm)	$60.
			Two Faced Bear	1994	9in (23cm)	$100.
272	Miki Saito	Kali Bears	Parade	1995	15-3/4in (40cm)	$300.
			Pablo	1995	23-3/4in (60cm)	$600.
			P.P. 150	1995	13in (35cm)	$200.
276	Tomoko Suenega	Jodie's Bears	Lapine	1995	3in (8cm)	$180.
277	Tomoko Suenaga	Jodie's Bears	Jo	1994	2in (5cm)	$100.
279	Masami Sugahara	My Own Teddy	Densuke	1994	10in (25cm)	$250.
			Noël	1994	11in (28cm)	$250.
281	Okiyasu Sugi	Gacha Gacha	Piewie	1994	15-3/4in (40cm)	$450.
282	Okiyasu Sugi	Gacha Gacha	Big Ear	1995	1in (3cm)	$150.
			York	195	2in (5cm)	$150.
			Honey	1995	1-1/2in (4cm)	$150.
			Jimmy	1995	1-1/2in (4cm)	$150.
283	Harumi Sugimoto		Cherry	1995	14in (36cm)	$200.
			Blueberry	1995	18in (46cm)	$300.
284	Harumi Sugimoto		Hope	1995	10in (25cm)	$200.
288	Yukie Tatsuki	Les NOUNOURS par Yuki	Cherry Babies	1995	3-4in (8-10cm)	$280. (set)
289	Yukie Tatsuki	Les NOUNOURS par Yuki	Cookie Faces	1995	4in (10cm)	$128.
			Cookie Faces	1995	16in (40cm)	$280.
291	Rie Watanabe	Own House	Mac	1995	4in (10cm)	$110.

NEW ZEALAND TEDDY BEAR ARTISTS

Illustration	Name of Artist	Company Name	Name of Bear	Year	Size	Price $
293	Helen Godfrey	Buzzbee Bears	Clown Teddy	1994	6in (15cm)	$45.
294	Syndi Muir	Muir Bears	Big Bear	1992	28in (71cm)	$325.
			Open Mouth	1994	11in (28cm)	$135.
			Cuddles	1995	17in (43cm)	$180.
295	Robin Rive	Countrylife New Zealand	McNaughty	1995	25in (64cm)	$174.
296	Robin Rive	Countrylife New Zealand	Matilda	1995	12-1/2in (32cm)	$40.
			Algeron	1994	12-1/2in (32cm)	$42.
			Chesterton	1994	17in (43cm)	$56.

SOUTH AFRICAN TEDDY BEAR ARTISTS

Illustration	Name of Artist	Company Name	Name of Bear	Year	Size	Price $
298	Eunice Beaton	Thread Bears	Bo	1995	23-3/4in (60cm)	$195.

SWISS TEDDY BEAR ARTISTS

Illustration	Name of Artist	Company Name	Name of Bear	Year	Size	Price $
300	René Tscherring	Pink Dino Bears	Ueli	1994	10in (25cm)	$152.

150

BERRYMAN'S INTERNATIONAL TEDDY BEAR ARTISTS AUCTION – 1996

Prices Realized

Berryman's International Teddy Bear Artists Auction was an international effort designed to raise funds by auctioning donated Teddy Bears. Its goal was to aid those who suffered from the tragic earthquake in Japan (January 17, 1995).

When I first heard the horrible news of the earthquake, my thoughts immediately went to all my Japanese friends and how I could possibly help them. Teddy Bears have long been acknowledged as a universal healing and consoling power; they have been successfully used for raising funds for many worthy causes around the world.

Knowing the "Power of the Teddy Bear," I contacted Teddy Bear artists and manufacturers around the world and invited them to help by donating a Teddy Bear for the auction.

Some of the best known and most-caring people in the Teddy Bear world also joined me to work on this worthy cause. My friends who jointed me in this project include: Gary and Mary Ruddell, publishers of Hobby House Press and Kazundo Onozuka, founder of the Japan Teddy Bear Association.

An event of this nature was never before held in Japan. It took place January 30, 1996 at the beautiful Tokyo Prince Hotel and raised ¥22 million (approximately $220,000), from the 131 Teddy Bear donations.

Below are a list of the donated bears (the majority of artist bears are one-of-a-kind) and the record breaking (charity) prices that were donated at Berryman's International Teddy Bear Artist Auction.

Illustration	Name of Artist	Company Name	Name of Bear	Size	Price (yen)	Price ($) Rate ¥100 per $
1	Sharon LaPointe	Enchanted Bears	The Jester	26in (66cm)	¥200,000	$2,000.
2	Robert Welch & Allen Chau	Whatabear	Reggie	25in (64cm)	¥95,000	$950
3	Fay Maloney	FayM	Matilda Ted & Kylic Koala on Walkabout	10-17in (25-43cm)	¥55,000	$550.
4	Mari and Akemi Koto	Koto Bears	Kabuto Bear Akira	14in (36cm)	¥200,000	$2,000.
5	Jo Greeno	Jo's Bear Emporium	Junior	12in (31cm)	¥200,000	$2,000.
6	Rosalie Frischmann	Mill Creek Creations	The Portrait	11-12in (28-56cm)	¥300,000	$3,000.
7	Christy Firmage	Christy's Bears	Sophie	12in (31cm)	¥100,000	$1,000.
8	Carol Stewart	Carol Stewart's Miniature Teddy Bears Inc.	Molly	8in (20cm)	¥200,000	$2,000.
9	April WhitcombGustafson		Priscilla Alden	3in (8cm)	¥160,000	$1,600.
10	Cheryl Augenstein	Belly Button Bears	Effie	24in (61cm)	¥90,000	$900.
11	Terumi Yoshikawa	Rose Bear	Proposal Bear	12in (31cm)	¥75,000	$750.
12	Barbara Golden	"Can't Bear To Part"	"One World"	14in (36cm)	¥320,000	$3,200.
13	Shirley Boyington	Bearington Bears	Fugika	28in (71cm)	¥100,000	$1,000.
14	Janie Comito	Janie Bear	Pansy Annas	1-3/8-4-1/2in (3-12cm)	¥130,000	$1,300.
15	Carol Lynn Rôssel Waugh	Yetta Bears	Carries' Cowgirl	16in (41cm)	¥95,000	$950.
16	Celia D. Baham	Celia's Teddies	Lavender	16in (41cm)	¥90,000	$900.
17	Monty and Joe Sours	The Bear Lady	Jackie	12in (31cm)	¥90,000	$900.
18	Cookie Mosley	Out of Hand Design	Madam Elaina Whitherford	9in (23cm)	¥100,000	$1,000.
19	Linda Spiegel-Lohre	Bearly There, Inc.	Paddie	14in (36cm)	¥140,000	$1,400.
20	Joan Woessner	Bear Elegance	Miss Bearington	26in (66cm)	¥120,000	$1,200.
21	Sayuri "Saki" Romerhaus	Romerhaus Creations	Flying Home	1-1/2in (4cm)	¥230,000	
22	Barbara Sixby	Zucker Bears	The Zucker Fire Department	10-20in (25-51cm)	¥300,000	$3,000.
23	Beverly White	Happy Tymes	Berryman's Bear "Ready For the Festivities"	16in (41cm)	¥1,000,000	$10,000.
24	Michi Takahashi	Fairy Chuckle	Over the Rainbow		¥700,000	$7,000.
25	Regina Brock	Regina Brock Bears	Brock	22in (56cm)	¥230,000	$2,300.
26	Sue and Randall Foskey	The Nostalgic Bear Co.	Prissy Priscilla and Her Bear Purse	20in (51cm)	¥200,000	$2,000.
27	Gisele Nash	Cinnamon Bears and Friends	Seasoned Citizen	11in (28cm)	¥80,000	$800.
28	Octavia Chin	"O" Bears	Wee and Me	3/4-2-1/4in (2-6cm)	¥250,000	$2,500.
29	Barbara Conley	Roley Bear Company	Teddi	16-1/2in (42cm)	¥330,000	$3,300.
30	Michelle Province	Itty Bitty Small Originals	Forest Friends	1-7/8-4-3/8in (5-11cm)	¥300,000	$3,000.
31	Dee Hockenberry	Bears 'N Things	Kobe Rose	13in (33cm)	¥65,000	$650.
32	Pat Lyons	Free Spirit Bears	Medicine Flower	14in (36cm)	¥60,000	$600.
33	Rhoda Curtis	Lending a Helping Hand Through Caring Hearts		4in (10cm)	¥80,000	$800.
34	Rita Loeb	Rita Loeb's Tiny Teddy Co.	Reginald	4-1/2in (12cm)	¥60,000	$600.
35	Flore Mediate	Flora's Teddies	Charlie	22in (56cm)	¥230,000	$2,300.
36	Luwana Eldridge	Kare 'N' Love Bears 'Future Antiques'	Mahealani and Lani	3-1/2-7in (9-18cm)	¥55,000	$550.
37	Joyce Haughey	Bearcraft	Kim	26in (66cm)	¥250,000	$2,500.
38	Sue Coe	Bear Feet	Unity	20in (51cm)	¥80,000	$800.
39	Anne-Marie van Gleder	Sunny Bears Holland	Whisty	16in (41cm)	¥90,000	$900.
40	Lisa Lloyd	Bears by Lloyd	Pamela	2-5/8in (7cm)	¥60,000	$600.
41	Lyda Rijs-Gertenbach	Lyda's Bear	Nora	6in (15cm)	¥170,000	$1,700.
42	Jeanette Warner	Nette Bears	Teddy and Pin Pal	5-25in (13-64cm)	¥800,000	$8,000.
43	Atsuko Takahashi	A.T. Bears	Limes	4-1/4in (11cm)	¥130,000	$1,300.
44	Jonette Stabbert	Poppette Doll Studio	Gulden	4-1/2in (10cm)	¥50,000	$500.
45	Serieta Harrell	Sersha Collectibles	Beth Ann	18in (46cm)	¥70,000	$700.
46	Ginger Brame	The Piece Parade	Pee Wee Teddy Bee	3-1/4in (8cm)	¥100,000	$1,000.
47	Robert Raikes	Raikes Originals	Bobbie	24in (61cm)	¥1,100,000	$11,000.
48	Helen and Roger Morris	Factoria Toyworks	Golli and Berry	2-3/4-7in (7-18cm)	¥350,000	$3,500.
49	Flore Emory	Flore Bears	Happy and Friend	11-16in (28-41cm)	¥850,000	$8,500.
50	Mayumi Watanabe	Mammie Bear	Birdie	10in (25cm)	¥100,000	$1,000.
51	Renee Casey	Renee's Bears& Other Things	Mercy	4-1/2in (12cm)	¥110,000	$1,100.
52	Karla Mahanna	Karla Mahanna Artist Bears	Bongles	16in (41cm)	¥110,000	$1,100.
53	Henk van der Vrande	Nosy Bears	Jingle	17in (43cm)	¥200,000	$2,000.
54	Willy Sengers-van der Vrande	Bear With Me	Bell	14in (35cm)	¥80,000	$800.

151

Illustration	Name of Artist	Company Name	Name of Bear	Size	Price (yen)	Price ($) Rate ¥100 per $
55	Nan Wright	Olde Tyme Toys and Treasures	Faith and Hope	10in (25cm)	¥160,000	$1,600.
56	Sarah McClellan	Sal's Pals	Antiqued Teddy	16in (41cm)	¥280,000	$2,800.
57	Marie Zimmerman	Paw Quette	Cherry Blossom	17in (43cm)	¥120,000	$1,200.
58	Corla Cubillas	The Dancing Needle	Two's Company	12-19in (31-48cm)	¥700,000	$7,000.
59	Kelli Kilby	Kelli's Kollectibles	Kibi San and Kuma Chan	2-3in (5-8cm)	¥320,000	$3,200.
60	Peggy Baughman	Pinewood Designs	Markus	13in (33cm)	¥70,000	$700.
61	Althea Leistikow	Bears by Althea	Miss Suzanne	9in (23cm)	¥80,000	$800.
62	Billee Henderson	Billee's Beasties	Mr. Magic	17in (43cm)	¥340,000	$3,400.
63	Gloria Franks	Goose Creek	Joy	23in (58cm)	¥160,000	$1,600.
64	Wanda Shope	Wandabears	Faith Brings Hope	7-28in (18-71cm)	¥190,000	$1,900.
65	Kathleen Wallace	Stier Bears	Liam and Wesley	10-17in (25-43cm)	¥550,000	$5,500.
66	Cindy Martin	Yesterbears	Clown Yesterbear	28in (71cm)	¥250,000	$2,500.
67	Lynn Lumley	Grandma Lynn Teddy Bears	Craig and Roman Paul	5-14in (13-36cm)	¥250,000	$2,500.
68	Anouk Johanna	Wearable Bears	Prince Quimby	1-3/4in (5cm)	¥53,000	$530.
69	Betsy Reum	Bears-in-the-Gruff	Fuschia	20in (51cm)	¥260,000	$2,600.
70	John Blackburn	Canterbury Bears Ltd.	Flash	33in (84cm)	¥100,000	$1,000.
71	Kazumi Shoji	Browny Bear	Mika	7in (18cm)	¥102,000	$1,020.
72	Mike Freeland	Refracted Reflections	Peri	8in (20cm)	¥200,000	$2,000.
73	Val Freeland	Refracted Reflections	Queen of Heart	16in (41cm)	¥130,000	$1,300.
74	Kathy LacQuay	Bearkins	Red Cloud	2-3/4in (7cm)	¥135,000	$1,350.
75	Terase Ng		Iris Fairy	1-3/4in (5cm)	¥85,000	$850.
76	Karen Rundlett	Karen's Creations	Bonnie-Sue	16-1/2in (42cm)	¥170,000	$1,700.
77	Evelyn Penfield	Penfield Bear Stores	Sammy	4-1/2in (10cm)	¥60,000	$600.
78	Norma Thomas		Teddy's Tea Time	3in (8cm)	¥95,000	$950.
79	Stacey Stucky	Tattered Ear Bear & Toy Works	Popples	3-1/2in (8cm)	¥110,000	$1,100.
80	Donna Hodges	Bearons of La Jolla	Snow Bear	20in (51cm)	¥230,000	$2,300.
81	Pauline Weir	We're Bears	Tracy	4-1/2in (12cm)	¥65,000	$650.
82	Debra Bedwell-Koontz	D'Bears	Navajo Bear	21in (51cm)	¥190,000	$1,900.
83	Genie Buttita	Genie B's Bears	Sara and Baby Bear	2-1/4-5in (6-13cm)	¥290,000	$2,900.
84	Diane Gard	A Bear With A Heart	Gabriella	32in (81cm)	¥180,000	$1,800.
85	Dagmar Strunck	"Barenhohle"	Waltzing Matilda	15in (38cm)	¥300,000	$3,000.
86	Beverly Matteson-Port	Beverly Port Originals	Beverly's Bébé Rosette	14in (36cm)	¥90,000	$900.
87	Tammy Torrence	Tammy Torrence Teddy's	Ted E. Bear	4in (10cm)	¥85,000	$850.
88	Sally Winey	Winey Bears	Sally's Bear	17in (43cm)	¥60,000	$600.
89	Steve Schutt	Bear- "S" -ence	Doodles	12in (31cm)	¥270,000	$2,700.
90	Samantha Fredericks	Bliss Toys	Carl	13in (33cm)	¥56,000	$560.
91	Robin Rive	Countrylife New Zealand	Jo Bear	25in (64cm)	¥280,000	$2,800.
92	Howard and Karen Calvin	Ballard Baines	Ah Poo!	8in (20cm)	¥220,000	$2,200.
93	Susan Vejtasa	Golden Harlequin Bears	Lady Jane	16in (41cm)	¥85,000	$850.
94	Judy Ahrend	Ahrend Heirloom Bears	Fuji San	10in (25cm)	¥240,000	$2,400.
95	Kumiko Komuchi	K and K Bears	Propose	2in (5cm)	¥85,000	$850.
96	Ted Menten		Lady Kobe	26in (66cm)	¥160,000	$1,600.
97	Denis Shaw	Denis's Den	Ononata, the "Bear-fly"	12in (31cm)	¥85,000	$850.
98	Ho Phi Le		Ho's Bear		¥50,000	$500.
99	Ikuyo Kasuga	Bruin	Pyjama Party	12in (28cm)	¥70,000	$700.

Copies of Berryman's International Teddy Bear Artist Auction catalog may be purchased at $5.00 from:
Hobby House Press, Inc., One Corporate Drive, Grantsville, Maryland 21536 • (800) 554-1447

UNCATALOGUED BERRYMAN'S AUCTION BEARS

Lot No.	Name of Artist	Manufacturer	Name of Bear	Price ¥	Price ($)
1001		Schuco	Tricky Bear	¥35,000	$350.
1002		Bing	Mini Bear	¥70,000	$700.
1003		Bing	Grandma Bear	¥57,000	$570.
1004		Bing	Banker Bear	¥27,000	$270.
1005		Bing	Cave Bear	¥56,000	$560.
1006		Clemens	Charcoal Bear	¥25,000	$250.
1007		Steiff	Compass Bear	¥97,000	$970.
1008		Annalee	Ballerina	¥18,000	$180.
1009	Robert Raikes	Robert Raikes	Bride & Groom	¥105,000	$1050.
1010	Terry & Doris Michaud	The Michaud Collection	Aunt Eunice	¥43,000	$430.
1011	Terry & Doris Michaud	The Michaud Collection	Just Ted	¥33,000	$330.
1012	North American Bear Co.		Dorothy & Toto	¥27,000	$270.
1013	North American Bear Co.		Baseball Boy	¥30,000	$300.
1014	Bearly People		Lady Frances	¥30,000	$300.
1015	Mary Meyers		Rose	¥42,000	$420.
1016	Carol Black	Bearhearts U.S.A.	Victoria Rose	¥42,000	$420.
1017	John Renpenning		Billy	¥54,000	$540.
1018	Hermann (donated by Susan Wiley)		Zotty 1950 (16in)	¥72,000	$720.
1019	Hermann (donated by Susan Wiley)		Zotty 1950 (18in)	¥63,000	$630.
1020			Holly Bears	¥55,000	$550.
1021	Kaylee Nilan	Beaver Valley		¥78,000	$780.
1022	Charleen Kinser Designs	Forever Toys		¥120,000	$1,200.
1023		Cooperstown Bears	Cooperstown Teddy	¥110,000	$1,100.
1024		Merrythought	Martha	¥55,000	$550.
1025	Bonnie J. Hotchikin		"Pom-Pom the Clown"	¥170,000	$1,700.
1026		Hermann		¥170,000	$1,700.
1027	Terumi Yoshikawa	Rose Bear	Ichiro	¥350,000	$3,500.
1029	Steiff		Harrods Centenary Bear	¥60,000	$600.
1030	Masako Kuroyanagi		Marcel (Penguin Bear)	¥400,000	$4,000.
1031	Steiff		Taro-1	¥60,000	$600.
1032	Steiff		Taro-2	¥55,000	$550.
1033	Elke Block		Ani To Imouto	¥140,000	$1,400.

152